RADIOHEAD

HYSTERICAL & USELESS
REVISED & UPDATED
MARTIN CLARKE

PLEXUS
LONDON

ACKNOWLEDGEMENTS

We would like to thank the following photographers
and photo agencies:

Cover photograph by Steve Double/SIN

Steve Double/Retna; Pat Pope/Retna; Jay
Blakesberg/Retna; David Tonge, Matt Anker/Retna;
Niels Van Iperen/Retna; Steve Granitz/Retna; Youri
Lenquette/Retna; Steve Double/SIN; Piers
Allardyce/SIN; Andy Willsher/SIN; Roy Tee/SIN; EMI
Records UK/Tom Sheehan/Parlophone; Tony Kelly/All
Action; Gene Weatherley/All Action; Andy
Willsher/All Action; Benoit Peverelli/Camera Press;
Dennis Morris; Ken Sharp.

Special thanks to Ronan Munro of Nightshift for
loaning material; and to Ken Sharp for his photographs
of Radiohead in the recording studios;

Thanks to Max Kolombos for compiling the
discography.

RADIOHEAD
RADIOHEAD
RADIOHEAD
RADIOHEAD
RADIOHEAD
RADIOHEAD
RADIOHEAD
RADIOHEAD
RADIOHEAD
RADIOHEAD
RADIOHEAD
RADIOHEAD

RADIOHEAD
HYSTERICAL & USELESS
REVISED & UPDATED
MARTIN CLARKE

RADIOHEAD
RADIOHEAD
RADIOHEAD
RADIOHEAD
RADIOHEAD
RADIOHEAD

contents

< c h a p t e r : 1 >

WE'RE TOO YOUNG TO FALL ASLEEP

'My mother has always said that I was a very a happy kid who just worked all the time. Using my hands. Building stuff out of Lego, taking out my bike – I was obsessed with my bike – riding that and drawing cars. Then when I discovered rock 'n' roll it was designing and drawing guitars. I never got bored as a kid. Never ever. I wanted to build bridges. I had this wicked Ladybird book of bridges . . . I didn't get kicked around as a kid. Sorry to disappoint.' **Thom**

MUCH has been made of Thom Edward Yorke's supposedly stressful, bullied childhood. It is claimed that he endured various traumas that were to fester inside him until they emerged in Radiohead's lyrics, which drip with repressed angst.

It is true that some elements of Thom's childhood did indeed cause him some distress, but not as this amateur psychology suggests. A certain instability was caused by his family uprooting themselves a couple of times and relocating – the first of these came shortly after his birth on 7 October 1968 in Wellingborough, Northamptonshire, when his family moved to Scotland, due to his father's job selling chemical engineering equipment. Quite early on it became apparent that Thom not only had a frail physique but also an introverted personality. These concerned his father, who had been a champion boxer at university. He made some well-intended efforts to toughen up his son, but they were doomed to failure; at one point he bought some boxing gloves for Thom, but every time he playfully hit him, he would just fall over.

However, Thom's biggest problem was a lazy eye, which he had from birth. When it became clear that the condition would not clear up of its own accord, plans were made to operate, by grafting a muscle on to the damaged eyelid. By the age of six, Thom had undergone five such operations, but unfortunately the final surgery was rather imprecise, and he was left with a permanently paralysed, slightly drooping eyelid. To make matters worse, the hospitals he attended did little to accommodate a child's sensitivities – he recalled frightened nights sleeping in wards next to geriatric wings, where senile old men talked to themselves or vomited in the corridors. The provision of only a radio, and no television or phones, made the young Thom dread each visit to the hospital even more. Emotionally unsettled by the experience and physically deformed because of its failure, Thom now looks back on these years with little relish: 'Hospitals are fucking horrifying places.' He has also said, 'I went half blind. I can kind of see. I can judge if I'm going to hit something but that's just about it.'

'It was a very malicious school and everyone had malicious nicknames, so Salamander was par for the course.'

For the first year of his primary education, Thom was forced to wear an eye-patch for recuperative purposes. Needless to say, this instantly became the source of amusement among his unforgiving peers, and throughout his early childhood he found himself the victim of many a playground joke. His disfigurement prompted dozens of suitably cruel nicknames, the most popular being Salamander. Inevitably, Thom reacted and tried to defend himself – he later recalled to *Vox* how he 'got into a fight with the guy who originated the name, but that didn't stop it. It was a very malicious school and everyone had malicious nicknames, so Salamander was par for the course.'

This hostility did not stop him developing a crush on one of his classmates, and much to his surprise, she reciprocated: 'My first french kiss . . . I was seven, she was my first girlfriend. We were in the playground and we promised to get married straight afterwards. But then I moved away from Scotland, where

I lived, and never saw her again . . . she probably doesn't remember me at all, but I remember her. Her name was Kate Ganson, and her Dad had a great Lotus car.' The move, again because of his father's job, was to Oxford. Joining the Standlake Church of England School as a new boy meant he was now subjected to a fresh ordeal of abuse and hectoring from new persecutors.

However, away from his troublesome school life, Thom had his music which he had always loved. Directly attributing his creativity to his mother's personality (saying that he had inherited his hyperactivity from his father), from an early age he had shown a particular aptitude for music. This was encouraged by his parents who bought him a Spanish guitar for his eighth birthday. Learning how to play it was painstakingly slow, and after six months all he had to show for his efforts was a rather clumsy rendition of 'Kumbaya'.

'It was a very musical school, but I was surrounded by all these kids who said, "Yeah, we like rock music – the Beatles and Simon and Garfunkel," that kind of crap.'

After several years spent aping Brian May in front of his bedroom mirror, Thom's not inconsiderable energies inevitably turned to forming his own band, but tellingly this would be no ordinary four-piece guitar band. Instead, an eleven-year-old Thom formed a bizarre duo with a school friend, and they started to write their own material immediately. Their chief performance consisted of Thom squealing away painfully on a cheap guitar while his colleague re-wired television sets in the background, which generally exploded. Their only recognisable melody was a track called 'Mushroom Cloud' which ruminated on the evils of the atomic explosion, and in particular, 'more about how it looked than how terrible it was'. Thom also remembered that in rehearsal they would 'make a lot of noise then go and drive Morris Minors round his garden.'

By the time Thom graduated as a day boy at the all-boys Abingdon public school near Oxford, he had already started to sing along to his own compositions. He was, by now, collating a sizeable record collection of his own, cluttering his bedroom with albums by a diverse array of musicians such as Magazine, Joy Division and the punk poet John Cooper Clarke. As early as his first year at school, Thom became aware of the myopia that often surrounds music: 'It was a very musical school, but I was surrounded by all these kids who said, "Yeah, we like rock music – the Beatles and Simon and Garfunkel," that kind of crap. Or even worse, they were into Mozart and Enya. You played them Joy Division and they'd say, "Oh no, he's out of tune, isn't he?"' Undeterred by this rather conservative environment, Thom spent many hours ensconced deep in the quiet maze of music rooms, where the isolation of the sound-proofed cubicles provided welcome respite from the distractions around him. His fascination blossomed, as did his developing talent.

Thom was only 5' 5", although after Ed's chiropractor father treated him in late 1997, he grew an inch!

He naturally gravitated towards like-minded boys in his school, and it was through this that he first met the future members of Radiohead. Thom ingratiated himself into the school punk band, TNT, where he joined forces with Colin Greenwood. Thom immediately took up vocal duties, 'because no-one else would' (with a microphone stuck to the end of a broom handle), and struck up a close friendship with Colin. After only a few months, TNT's lack of ambition and original material drove a disillusioned Thom to leave, and he was followed shortly after by Colin, who was keen to continue working with his diminutive friend. (Thom was only 5' 5", although after Ed's chiropractor father treated him in late 1997, he grew an inch!) Colin, an Oxford native and budding bassist, was in the same year at school as Thom but was nine months younger. Together they would attend school parties, Colin adorned in a catsuit and beret, Thom in a garish crushed velvet dinner suit, frilly blouse and heavy duty mascara, where they would hijack the record player and spin Joy Division and Magazine songs. Needless to say, they were not the most popular boys at school. One teacher remembers how 'they were the sort of computer nerds of that day and age. They just sat in their room thrashing away at their guitars all day. Everyone just thought they were weird, especially Thom.'

Such musical unorthodoxy soon introduced the pair to Oxford-born Ed

O'Brien, also in their year, the son of a doctor and solidly middle-class. Ed had met Colin before, at a school production of Gilbert and Sullivan's *Trial By Jury*. Ed's first recollection of Thom was when they were both involved in a school play, Ed as an actor and Thom as part of the musical accompaniment. As Ed later recalled: 'There was this tense dress rehearsal, and Thom and this other fella were jamming free-form cod-jazz throughout it. The director stopped the play and shouted up to this scaffold tower thing they were playing on, trying to find out what the hell was going on. Thom started shouting down, "I don't know what the fuck we're supposed to be playing." And this was to a teacher.' Thom's reasons for choosing Ed are famously rather more blunt – 'because he looked liked Morrissey'.

At first, this newly formed threesome rehearsed with the aid of a cheap drum machine, whose rudimentary programming provided adequate, albeit rather limiting, rhythmic backing. Unfortunately, the machine soon broke down and lack of funds forced the fledgling band to look for a human replacement. Enter Phil Selway, born in Hemingford Grey, Cambridgeshire. 'We were all scared of Phil,' Colin later recalled to writer Clare Kleinedler, 'He was in the class ahead of us, and he was in this band called Jungle Telegraph, so we knew him as 'The Graf'. We weren't old enough and not in with his crowd.' To make matters worse, some of Phil's friends regularly beat them up.

Nevertheless, circumstances demanded that this potential recruit be approached, and so after much procrastination a meeting was arranged in a local pub and Ed was lumbered with the task of speaking to Phil. Full of teenage bravado, Ed told how he flustered his way through the meeting: 'I was a bit scared going up to him . . . It was quite like a scene from *Grease*. I was like "Um, so, how's it going?" And Phil was like, "O.K. How was your gig last night?" And I said, "Yeah, cool, man. We had a bit of trouble with the drum machine." Phil says, "Yeah." And I say, "We're rehearsing next week. Wanna make it?"' Suitably impressed by this falsely laid-back offer, Phil agreed to try out a rehearsal. When the time came, Thom was apparently not intimidated by him – at that first rehearsal he listened to Phil's drumming and then asked, 'Can't you play any fucking faster?'

The first public airing of the new line-up enjoyed what must qualify as the longest debut gig in history – 24 hours! Their almost entirely improvised performance was part of a school marathon, during which the only recognisable offering was a dire but well-intended version of 'Dear Prudence', the Beatles track which had recently been covered by Siouxsie and the Banshees.

'They thought I was going to turn into a drug-taking lunatic from hell, and that was the end of me.'

Although the school was all boys, social contact with the opposite sex was not impossible. Thom recalled in *Vox*: 'When I was about 15, me and my friends invited these girls round. We were in the bogs – smoking, drinking and generally having a good time – when this right cunt of a teacher caught us. He made us phone our parents and say exactly what we had done, and said we were going to be expelled. It wasn't a big deal, but it completely destroyed my parents. They thought I was going to turn into a drug-taking lunatic from hell, and that was the end of me. We never even got suspended in the end, the guy was just winding us up. Arsehole.'

Another factor that has often been cited as inspiration for Thom's strained lyrics is his hatred for his headmaster at school (as he later made clear in his song 'Bishop's Robes'). Although Thom is reluctant to over-emphasise this, he has made no secret of his feelings for a person he considered a megalomaniac. At one stage, a school punk band played a gig that got a little out of hand, as a consequence of which the headmaster banned all pop music. He also turned down repeated requests from Thom for his band to play a gig at school. Sometimes the width of the boys' trouser bottoms was measured to make sure they were not the fashionable drainpipes, although the same strict rules did not seem to apply to the headteacher's own sartorial tastes: 'He started walking around in bishop's clothing . . . . and he started preaching in the school assembly, even though he wasn't ordained or anything, and he started forcing people to go to chapel. This was the guy that I focused most of my teenage hatred on. I still hate him and if I see or hear of him I get this deep sinking feeling . . . That sort of bloke, a total bloody nut.' Thom would often skip classes and walk around the town centre, where he got himself into fights, although 'they really weren't fights, because the other guys'd hit me and I'd fall over'.

The band's line-up was bolstered (at the time no-one could have imagined exactly to what degree) when Colin's younger brother Jonny joined. Two school years younger than the others, Jonny was already a gifted, self-taught guitarist by the age of fourteen, having been introduced to music largely through his older

An early Radiohead press shot.

sister's ceaseless playing of Magazine albums. As a six-year-old he had bought his first record, a pink vinyl copy of Squeeze's 'Cool For Cats', which he recited word for word to the bewildered dinner ladies at school. As a teenager he bought a Rickenbacker, enamoured by the likes of Johnny Marr, Paul Weller and Peter Buck, and disdainful of the cock-rock Stratocaster antics of the more clichéd lead guitarists. Within three months he had complemented his six-string with an array of effects pedals – distortion, phaser, delay – and had started to experiment with the enormous palette of sounds this set-up offered him.

Jonny plundered the family archives in search of suitably musical ancestors, but was dismayed to find that apart from a grandfather who had briefly taken up the euphonium, he appeared to be the only musician other than Colin. Their mother was completely tone deaf. Undeterred, Jonny quickly developed into a multi-instrumentalist of some ability: he played jazz piano, recorder, viola, violin and regularly performed in the Thames Valley Youth Orchestra. However, Jonny knew that his credentials alone were hardly likely to win him a place in his brother's rock band, which he watched with an increasingly envious eye. Legend has it he would turn up to band rehearsals with a multitude of different instruments, each one a vain attempt to impress his friends into letting him join.

The established theory has it that Jonny's first performance with the band was at the infamous Jericho Tavern. This venue formed the nucleus of the Oxford scene at the time, and hosted scores of early gigs by bands such as Ride, Supergrass, Slowdive and Radiohead. At this particular show, Jonny apparently sat longingly by the side of the stage with his harmonica, until Thom gestured for him to climb up and join in. Jonny remembers events somewhat differently: 'It was a Sunday morning, and I had stayed at a friend's house the night before . . . I was about fourteen years old and we were just watching videos and talking about girls and things. And I got a call from my lovely brother Colin. "We're rehearsing near where you are now. Have you got your harmonica?" I said "yes", and he said, "Well come down right now." So I went over . . . that was the first time really. It was loud and rackety and noisy as hell. It was pretty cool then.' One week later came the aforementioned gig at the Jericho Tavern, when a desperate Jonny was finally welcomed into the fold. Thom's recollection of their first time with Jonny was less clear: 'I don't remember the first time, really, I just remember it was the only time I used to get girls. They used to come to our rehearsals.'

Jonny's mother watched her son's involvement in the band with growing concern. After losing their father at a young age, Colin and Jonny's mother was naturally very protective of her two young boys, and she worried about the effects of this musical distraction on their school work – Jonny was highly intellectual, and Colin was already being cited as an academic of considerable potential. Thom's parents were also far from keen on his chosen hobby, so whenever he had a gig he would tell them he was staying over at a friend's house.

Part of Jonny's fascination was the material that Thom was producing – even at this early stage – he has since described the style as 'schizophrenic'. One track called 'Rattlesnake' consisted almost entirely of a single drum loop that Thom had crudely recorded on his home tape player, with some bad scratching over the top and some pseudo-Prince vocals. Another Waterboys-inspired song called 'The Chains' featured a viola, and was in sharp contrast to 'What Is That You See' which was little more than a feedback frenzy. 'I'd heard tapes of Thom's songs before I joined,' Jonny later told the media, 'and I couldn't get over the fact that if I played an Elvis Costello record and then his stuff, the songs were as good. And yet he was sixteen and at my school. A handful of those songs would stand up today.'

Calling themselves On A Friday, after the day of the week when they usually rehearsed, the band began gigging. One of their early gigs was at an open-air festival, where Colin noticed several couples apparently copulating on the grass. 'I like to think it was down to the seductive qualities of our music but I'd say had more to do with the vast quantities of beer that'd been consumed.' At this stage, Jonny's harmonica playing was fairly rudimentary, and his keyboard skills were initially so bad that they turned his volume off at some shows. He was struggling to find his role in the band, until one day after several months 'I came stumbling out with a guitar in my hand.'

Rehearsals were chaotic affairs, with the band struggling through almost every musical genre, including rock, ska, punk and country. Early shows saw the line-up swelled by a duo of saxophone playing sisters, who were so physically intimidating that they rapidly silenced any hecklers in the audience. These girls did not stay in the band for long, but inspired by Magazine, Joy Division and especially Talking Heads, On A Friday now had the truncated line-up and the growing confidence to pursue their rampant ambitions.

< chapter: 2 >

HERE WE ARE WITH OUR RUNNING AND CONFUSION

'I just think that people get up too early to leave houses where they don't want to live, to drive to jobs where they don't want to be in, in one of the most dangerous forms of transport on earth. I've never gotten used to that.' **Thom**

WITH growing parental concern at the musical distraction, it was with much relief that, in 1987, just when On A Friday had started to gel, Thom, Colin and Ed left school and went their separate ways in pursuit of futher education. As a result, between 1987 and 1991, the band's existence was reduced to the occasional gig snatched during breaks between terms. Colin had fulfilled his academic potential by winning a place at Cambridge University studying English, while Phil had already been reading the same subject for a year at Liverpool University. Ed started on a Politics degree at Manchester, and Jonny was still at school. This just left Thom.

Thom opted to take a year out before going to university. Taking a job selling mens' suits, he found himself once again consumed with hatred for one of his superiors, this time the shop floor manager. Thom's lack of patience with his customers was aggravated by the knowledge that he couldn't afford any of the suits he was selling – instead, he turned up for work in a smart second-hand outfit he had proudly bought from the town's Oxfam shop. This, along with his long and unkempt blond hair, did little to impress his boss, who Thom thought made it his mission to inconvenience and persecute him as often as possible. When asked why he hadn't sold any suits, Thom would reply, 'Because they're crap and nobody wants to buy them.' Matters came to a head when Thom was accused of allegedly stealing some stock, and he immediately handed in his notice. One small incident also occurred during this year, when Thom was working in a bar, which he always remembers: 'This madwoman came in and said, "You have beautiful eyes but they're completely wrong." Whenever I get paranoid, I just think about what she said.'

'I couldn't paint. I'm a bit clumsy. I did a few things on computer, but most of the time I was busy bragging about my future as a pop star.'

After another job working as an orderly in a mental hospital (which later became the inspiration for the skull-crushing song 'Climbing Up The Walls'), Thom finally made it to university, going to Exeter to study Fine Art and Literature. He admitted that he was a little surprised to be there at all, claiming that 'I couldn't paint. I'm a bit clumsy. I did a few things on computer, but most of the time I was busy bragging about my future as a pop star. My sketchbooks were full of lyrics and designs for record sleeves.' Largely uninterested in academia, he quickly became embroiled in the techno and house music scenes that spread across the country at the turn of the decade. Appearing regularly as a DJ at parties and small venues, he also temporarily joined a techno band called Flickernoise, 'a computer-with-dreadlocks band'. As with many of his peers, he drank far too often and far too much, until he was shaken out of this phase by a bout of alcohol poisoning. When he wasn't drinking or playing music, Thom would walk to the centre of town and sit for hours watching people, something that he still likes to do. Although he was far from being an outsider, Thom never felt fully comfortable with the hordes of self-important undergraduates who flooded the town every year: 'I was embarrassed to be a student,' he later told the press, 'because of what the little fuckers got up to. Walking down the street to be confronted by puke and shopping trolleys and police bollards. Fucking used to think, "No wonder they hate us." If I was going to throw up I did it in the privacy of my own room.'

Unfortunately, Thom himself was once the victim of the tension that so often exists between students and locals. He had taken to dressing as an old man, wearing a full-length overcoat and old-fashioned hat. While he was walking through Exeter, three 'townies' started mocking him so Thom turned to face them and blew them a kiss. Pulling sticks out from their own overcoats, they beat him senseless. Since then, his dress sense has been toned down a little!

Another incident saw Thom attend what he later described as 'the best party he had ever been to'. He was given an invite to go to a designated spot where he joined a large group of students who headed off to a field. On arrival, they all piled into an old battered car, in which they rolled down a steep hill. After several fairly spectacular crashes, the car was dismantled and makeshift musical instruments were fashioned out of it. A Chinese dragon was then made out of the remaining parts and the by-now thoroughly drunken students danced around camp fires they had lit. 'We crashed out in the open in our sleeping bags and I was awoken at seven by the smell of bacon and some loon with a megaphone shouting "Wake up, time to die!" That was pretty cool.'

While Thom was enjoying such pagan pursuits, the rest of On A Friday had joined various university bands, including outfits called King of Thailand, Shindig and Headless Chicken. Colin was fairly heavily involved in the Cambridge university music scene, getting himself elected as entertainments officer and promptly booking bands he knew (or was in) for rather excessive fees. However, despite the geographical separation and musical inactivity of On A Friday, the long term focus was never lost, and once its members who had gone to university had completed their respective courses, their next course of action was never open to debate. As Ed told Nancy Price: 'There was never any question that we weren't going to do it, really, in terms of making the effort . . . Looking back on it, what was amazing was the commitment. Ten years ago, we talked about it. We knew we wanted to do this.'

It was now the summer of 1991, and On A Friday were reconvened and recharged. While world domination awaited them, they wisely decided to get jobs in the meantime. Ed took up waiting tables in posh Oxford tea rooms full of tourists, Phil worked at a medical publishers and Thom spent a brief spell working in an architect's office. Colin seemed to land the best job – working behind the counter at the Oxford branch of Our Price records. As it turned out, this proved to be a pivotal move in Radiohead's career.

The reconvening of the group presented its youngest member, Jonny, with a agonising decision. He was only three months into a degree in music and psychology at Oxford Polytechnic when he was faced with leaving and joining the band. He went to ask his tutor to ask for advice, and was amazed to be told to go with the band. Much to his mother's horror, he did exactly this, although with the benefit of hindsight, he feels he has ironically made more of his education than he would have had he stayed at college: 'It's strange,' he told *Varsity*'s Tojvo Pajo, 'because I dropped out of music college to do this, and I'm finding myself now, using all that I was learning, probably more than if I'd stayed in college and tried to find a job afterwards.'

Unified by their mutual love of the band, Thom, Colin, Phil, Ed and Jonny did what thousands of bands before them have done (and regretted soon after) – they moved into a house together. Renting a semi-detached house near the centre of Oxford, the five of them rapidly reduced the previously presentable house to a tip. Musical instruments were strewn all over the house, the wallpaper was soon hanging off from being scratched by their gear, and the whole house had a coating of cigarette ash. Jonny never washed up, Colin bored everyone with his Pale Saints records and Thom annoyed the neighbours with his abrasive collection of hard house music.

Long evenings were spent crouched in the cold living room, flicking through their vast combined record collection, talking about their heroes and their own band. Interestingly, it was only Thom and Colin who really lasted the course in the house, feeding themselves on a diet of so-called 'pesto slop . . . idiot food' and scaring each other witless with tales of previous tenants: 'It was a bit eerie,' Colin told *Select*, 'because the woman who'd lived there before had died. I think she died in the house. And Ed and I kept finding things which had obviously belonged to her. Combs, half-empty fag packets, stuff like that. One day we found this half-eaten pork pie down the back of the sofa. It must've been there for months but you could still see the teeth marks. Of course, being morbid people we managed to convince ourselves that she'd choked on it.'

The five future members of Radiohead were the only legal tenants, but they let their friends wander in and out at will, so much so that the landlord did not actually know who lived there (a fact they found useful on rent days). Phil stayed there the least – he did have a room, but found the scummy conditions unbearable. In a fashion typical of Radiohead, even these extreme circumstances did little to incite rock 'n' roll behaviour, as Colin told *Select*: 'I think we spent most of the time trying to avoid each other as much as possible . . . The only other thing was that one day Phil came back and I'd eaten all his honey. I mean,

The Martyr's Memorial in Oxford was the setting for Radiohead's first photo session in late 1991.

the guy hadn't been there in weeks but still got really angry about it. He still brings it up to this day!'

Air FX and New Romantics are not two bands whose names will be forever etched into the Rock 'n' Roll hall of fame. They did, however, each contain a member who would prove to play a vital part in Radiohead's worldwide success – Chris Hufford and Bryce Edge. After the demise of their own eighties bands, the thirty-something partners set about establishing a complex of high-tech studios, workshops and business units in the small Oxfordshire village of Sutton Courtenay, not far from Abingdon, where their future charges had gone to school. Calling the project Courtyard Studios, Hufford and Edge's early optimism was soon battered by the stark reality of financial loss. From its inception in 1987, Courtyard struggled to survive, only occasionally buoyed by the sessions of the various Oxford bands from the thriving Thames Valley scene, with Slowdive's debut album in particular proving helpful. Almost inevitably, however, time and funds ran out and they were forced to dissolve the partnership. Choosing to continue in some form by renting the purpose-built studio from its new owner, Hufford and Edge set up their own production company to take advantage of the glut of talented local bands.

'It was a lot rougher, a lot punkier, quite frenetic and a faster tempo. But they were still very musical, the songs were well put together.'

One afternoon in late 1990, a friend of Hufford's assistant called John Butcher brought in a demo tape of On A Friday, which they had recorded the preceding April during the Easter vacation. It consisted of fifteen songs which were all roughly hewn and highly derivative. Hufford was impressed but only mildly: 'You couldn't hear any one band on it,' he later told Q magazine, 'There were some good tunes but it was all obviously ripped off mercilessly. [The last track] was a weird looped-up dance thing which was completely mental but had something about it that was very different. I asked if they had anything else. After about six months John brought in another tape with 'Stop Whispering', 'What Is It That You Say' and 'Give It Up' on it. These were great songs.

Now they had an identity' (even though 'Give It Up' contained the line 'Hey! give it up, oo-oh! Give it up, hey!'). He also said of the new material, 'It was a lot rougher, a lot punkier, quite frenetic and a faster tempo. But they were still very musical, the songs were well put together.'

On A Friday had been gigging relentlessly ever since their first post-graduation show at the Hollybush in Oxford, on 22 July 1991. Indeed, they had performed over 100 gigs before they gained any profile at all, including far from glamorous support slots to Dumpy's Rusty Nuts and Funking Barstewards. They were constantly writing new material as well, which explains the progression from the derivative first demo to that rather more refined and individual second tape that so interested Hufford. Curious and excited, he arranged to see On A Friday's next gig, at the Jericho Tavern, the very epicentre of the Oxford scene. That show changed his, and Radiohead's, life.

'I was completely and utterly blown away,' he later told *Q*. 'Out of all those Thames Valley bands of the time there were no performers or great singers but Thom was incredible. Brilliant songs with the amazing power of three guitars. I made a complete buffoon of myself, bursting backstage saying, "I've got to work with you!" I was so excited by them. They had fantastic energy. I could see it on a world level, even then.' He immediately offered to record their next demo at Courtyard, and On A Friday duly accepted.

From those sessions, which Hufford and Edge produced, the band delivered what has become known as the *Manic Hedgehog* tape, after the name of the key Oxford record store where you could buy demos by promising local bands. The tape included 'Nothing Touches Me', which Thom later explained was 'based on an artist who was imprisoned for abusing children and spent the rest of his life in a cell painting, but the song is about isolating yourself so much that one day you realise you haven't got any friends anymore and no one talks to you'. This track included lines such as 'I try to make her listen, when I turn away she's split.' Hufford and Edge were so convinced both by the tape and the band's live show that they offered to manage them as well, despite having no experience of this. Jonny's dismayed mother half-jokingly reacted to this news by claiming Hufford must be the 'son of Satan'.

Colin was still working in Our Price, and one of the record company sales reps who came in each week to offer him the latest releases was a man called Keith Wozencroft, a former musician from Gloucester who was now working for EMI. Keith had just got a new job as A&R for Parlophone, so Colin knew his next visit to the shop would be his last. With such a deadline, Colin mustered up the courage to proffer the *Manic Hedgehog* cassette to him, saying, 'You should sign my band . . . ' and invited him to their gig the following week. Wozencroft was interested and went to the open-air show which was in a nearby park at the end of October. Wozencroft told *Q*: 'There was no-one there in this little tent apart from a couple of their girlfriends. But they played really well. I left a message with the sound guy that it was great and kept in touch over the next few months.'

'Thom was like a little kid, having tantrums all over the stage. We shared the door money – we got about £30 each.'

At the same time, Bath Moles Club booker Jan Brown had passed the tape on to Charlie Myatt at the all-powerful ITB agency. He went to see a gig and liked them enough to start to find more shows for them. At one of these gigs, On A Friday were being supported by a band called Money For Jam, whose bassist Hannah Griffiths told *Mojo* magazine how: 'They had to use our drumkit, because theirs was in such a state. It was strange to see so many people turn up to see them. You could sense something was happening. Thom was like a little kid, having tantrums all over the stage. We shared the door money – we got about £30 each.'

Once he started working at Parlophone Wozencroft was eager to impress his new boss. There had already been a few whispers in the industry about On A Friday, so he decided to pursue them further, pencilling in their next gig, once more at the Tavern. The first tape he presented to his seniors was the *Manic Hedgehog* demo, and this, combined with their knowledge of Hufford and Edge's eighties bands (which had both been signed to Parlophone), resulted in the entire A&R team driving up to Oxford for this next show. Whereas Wozencroft had been a solitary industry figure at their previous gig, at the next show he was now shocked to find at least 25 record company scouts present, all of whom had paid to get in. Word had got out.

Up till now, On A Friday's reputation had largely been spread by their evocative and incendiary live show. Only a few days after the gig, the band also won their first magazine front cover, when the excellent and sadly now-defunct *Curfew* magazine plastered them across its front page. Inside, the editor explained how 'I finally realised what a great pop group they were at a pathetically attended gig at the Poly, with crap sound and a ludicrously curtailed set'. Thom then defended the band's often rather dour attitude by saying 'People sometimes say we take things too seriously, but it's the only way you'll get anywhere. We're not going to sit around and wait and just be happy if something turns up. We are ambitious. You have to be.'

There was now a very tangible sense of expectation about On A Friday's future. Wozencroft knew he had to act, and quickly (Island Records had rejected the demo tape, but only narrowly). An offer was made and the band accepted. So, on 21 December 1991, just over five months after Thom Yorke graduated from Exeter University, On A Friday signed a record deal with Parlophone for eight albums.

< c h a p t e r : 3 >

I GOT BETTER, I GOT BETTER, I GOT STRONG

'When we were off at college, Ride started up and the whole Thames Valley thing happened. By the time we got back it had all finished! That's called impeccable timing – we completely missed the boat!'
Thom

IN 1992, the Oxford-based band Ride released *Going Blank Again*, which critics saw as an unofficial epitaph for yet another dying music biz movement, the awkwardly christened 'The Scene That Celebrates Itself'. This had centred around a hub of bands who frequented various trendy London watering holes such as the Syndrome Club in Oxford Street on a Thursday night, the Powerhaus, the Underworld and the Borderline. The bands were often seen ligging at each other's gigs – Blur's studio party in Fulham to celebrate completing their debut album was attended by most of 'the scene's' leading lights. The range of bands included under this umbrella was wide and varied but was generally given to be listless, apolitical and monosyllabic groups who were fairly inactive live and had little to say in their music, which was often swathed in Dinosaur Jr/My Bloody Valentine nostalgic walls of noise, in sharp contrast to the decidedly bland lyrics. It was different to the baggy sound of 'Madchester', but it was not exactly life-affirming and eclectic. The scene even had an alternative monicker, 'shoe-gazing', a term invented by Andy Ross of Food Records to differentiate those bands from to his new charges Blur, although some journalists initially tried to include Damon Albarn's band in this group. Bands who were more accurately clustered together under this heading included Moose, Ride, the Boo Radleys, Lush, Chapterhouse, Telescopes and Slowdive.

More often than not, a band's inclusion was more to do with their ability to share a pint with a music journalist than with their musical affinity to the movement. Almost inevitably, the acclaim afforded to many of these bands began to ebb away after a while, and as it did their friendly associations turned into back-stabbing and mutual disregard, as bands desperately tried to avail themselves of the shoe-gazing millstone before it dragged them down with it. Not all of the 'shoe-gazers' lived past the scene, with only the Boo Radleys, Lush and Ride enjoying any further (albeit stunted) longevity.

On A Friday, geographically smack in the middle of what some called 'the Thames Valley scene' seemed willing and able to avoid any involvement totally, mostly because they were too busy at University to make the band a coherent force. Indeed, Thom was busy immersing himself in that other early nineties scene, house music. He went to raves, as did the other members, but never fully converted to the Summer of Love ethos. Jonny was similarly reluctant, telling *Raygun* , 'For the past few years, people got into raving, going to clubs, taking drugs and stuff like that. A lot of people believe they are going to have a better time taking drugs and raving than going to see a live band. I think that's rubbish.'

Even within Oxford, On A Friday were not really part of the scene. They did play a lot of gigs at the Jericho Tavern, they supped in the popular New Inn, and they frequented the Manic Hedgehog record store that was the nucleus of the local circuit, but they were always outsiders. Other bands like Ride, Slowdive and Swervedriver seemed to spearhead the movement, at times deliberately. On A Friday were never part of this scene, nor any other. Never would be.

'I remember when we first signed, someone said, "What agenda do you have?" With British bands, there was this whole thing about having something to say. But, maybe naively, we said, "It's about music." And that's what it's about.' **Ed O'Brien**

On A Friday travelled to London to meet the Parlophone team, and while they were sitting in the meeting, label head Rupert Perry stuck his head around the door and said 'You'll never see me again until you sell 500,000 units and then we'll shake hands and take a photo. By the way, I really like that song "Phillippa

Chicken", that's my favourite.' This track was also the latest On A Friday song to be deleted from their set (amongst other things, it contained some rather odd lyrics, including 'take me up to a warmer place, I got eggs, I got feathers, I got brains').

When the Sex Pistols first signed to A&M, they trashed the offices, pissed on the floor and shagged a secretary in the toilets. After their signing On A Friday travelled back up to Oxford and arranged to meet up for a celebratory drink in an hour or so. Unfortunately, the arrangements were far from clear, and they all spent the early evening wandering the rain-lashed streets of the town looking in vain for each other. Each eventually called it a day and went home on his own.

'A couple of weeks before the name change, we put on the radio in my car, and every channel was playing Michael Bolton, singing the same song. It was despicable. Satan had taken over the airwaves.'

The first thing On A Friday did on Parlophone was change their name. Their rather sixth-formish name had rightly come in for some criticism, so they finally agreed to change it after a particularly upsetting review in *NME* which called it 'a beer swilling Friday night moniker'. The new name of Radiohead was taken from a cod-reggae track on the Talking Heads *True Stories* album, of which they were all great fans. There had been other options, including Gravitate, Music (Greek spelling) and Jude. The latter was taken from the Thomas Hardy novel, *Jude The Obscure*, about a man vainly trying to get into Oxford university and driving himself insane in the process. 'Music' was their most pretentious option ('the most obnoxious thing you could possibly do'), fortunately ignored, but later used by another act. Thom later explained how they still love the connotations of the Radiohead name: 'Radiohead was cool and it is still cool because it just sums up all these these things about receiving stuff and . . . all these people in America have these teeth you can pick up radio on. They have this sort of metal in their teeth and some of them can pick up radio with it. I think that is very cool. And now of course they can implant things into your head that they can work and sort of observe your brain patterns. Radiohead is sort of . . . It's brilliant.' Jonny agreed: 'The radio is everywhere . . . I really hate the idea of radio waves being inescapable. Wherever you go, they're going through you. It's horrible.' Ed was a little more light-hearted about it, saying 'a couple of weeks before the name change, we put on the radio in my car, and every channel was playing Michael Bolton, singing the same song. It was despicable. Satan had taken over the airwaves.'

'The radio is everywhere . . . I really hate the idea of radio waves being inescapable. Wherever you go, they're going through you. It's horrible.'

With the name change complete, Radiohead returned to recording more demos with Hufford, and playing yet more gigs. British music journalist John Harris was persuaded by Hall Or Nothing (whom Parlophone had hired to do Radiohead's press) to see one of these, but, as he recalled later in Q, the bright new hopes were a mixed bag: 'News of their signing had spread and there was a real sense of expectation. They looked awful. Thom was wearing a brown crew-necked jumper, had cropped hair and looked very small, with none of the presence he has now. Musically they were all over the place. They started with something Rickenbackery that sounded like *All Mod Cons*-period jam, then they'd flip it with something that sounded like the Pixies. All the raw material was there but they hadn't found their feet stylistically.' Ian Gittins of *Melody Maker* was more enthusiastic, encouraged by the white noise created by Radiohead's three-guitar attack, saying, 'Radiohead are intriguing brooders. One to watch, I guess.'

Their first major-label release came in May 1992 with the four track *Drill* EP. The recording of this debut release had caused some degree of internal friction, as Chris Hufford and Bryce Edge elected themselves producers. Ironically, the duo had themselves suffered a similarly omnipotent managerial style when they were performers a decade previously, so in retrospect Hufford acknowledges this may not have been the wisest move: 'A huge conflict of interests. I think Thom was very unsure of my involvement . . . (and) I can be quite over-bearing and opinionated in the studio.'

Despite this, the debut effort was a solid starter. The lead track, 'Prove Yourself', opened with Thom's already highly distinctive and developed voice over a scratchy rhythm guitar, reminiscent of Billy Bragg's balladry, before crashing drums and guitars led off the rest of the song. The dynamic contrasts persisted, and the mixture of the melancholic and abrasive was compelling, although the structure was relatively orthodox. 'I can't afford to breathe in this town/nowhere to sit without a gun in my hand', laments Thom. In some ways, the track was similar to some of those of the so-called fraggle bands who were currently dominating the indie arena – Mega City Four, the Wonder Stuff and Ned's Atomic Dustbin for example – although Thom's voice clearly marked Radiohead out as very different indeed. This track contained the first of many classic Thom Yorke one-liners, when he sang 'I'm better off dead' (a lyric which was clearly lost on the Hospital Radio DJ in Newcastle, who was inadvertently playing the single dozens of times a week).

At times the EP was a little cluttered, and both 'Stupid Car' and 'You' left the listener with the feeling that the juddering rhythms and layered sonics sometimes muddied Radiohead's waters. At one point on 'You', there were even heavy metal guitars, and the lead melodies were never as strong as later material, but otherwise, and in the context of their career to date, this was a competent and strong release.

Despite BBC Radio 1's Gary Davies being a surprise fan and playing 'Prove Yourself' on his show, the release received very little fanfare elsewhere in the music press, perhaps the best, and most comic review being the one from an honest, albeit disorganised, journalist at *Melody Maker*. 'Having lost the press release for a white label, I can only be conjecture as to whether Radiohead is the band, the EP or the record company. Whichever, it's a bit of all right, kinda Husker Dü with gleeful harmonies, noisy guitars and an unapologetic fervour about something or other. Yeah.' While the music papers were quick to cite such fashionable American influences (they also readily mentioned the Pixies and the Throwing Muses), Thom preferred to think it was not so much the music, but the impact and attitude of American rock, and in particular its newly crowned kings Nirvana, that his band were trying to emulate: '"Smells Like Teen Spirit" had the kind of feel we're after. When it came on the radio, you had no choice but to listen to it. You couldn't just drive along and ignore it, it came out at you. I hope we'll come out of people's speakers in the same way. All our songs come from state of conflict, and if you listen to them in the right way, you're bound to feel that conflict as well.'

'Being onstage is the most important thing we do, everything else consists of waiting for that. It might sound old-fashioned, but we do try to give it everything.'

One feature of Radiohead's early days was their willingness to tour – during 1992 alone, they played 100 shows. For the *Drill* EP, they performed a series of small venue dates in the spring supporting the likes of Catherine Wheel, Machine Gun Feedback and the comic but short-lived ingenuity of the Sultans of Ping FC. Radiohead themselves had very little following, and poor organisation and low budgets meant that these first national tours were often not happy times. The most entertaining feature of the low-key dates was the crowd's participation in the 'I'm better off dead' line, screaming it back at the band.

However, Radiohead soon earned one of their first features in the weekly music press, namely a small article in the 'On' section of *NME*, next to a picture of the band, Phil still with some hair left, and Thom angrily throwing his middle finger up at the photographer. In another early piece in the press, the fresh band explain how 'when we're on stage it's almost like an exorcism – we really throw ourselves into what we play' and how 'being onstage is the most important thing we do, everything else consists of waiting for that. It might sound old-fashioned, but we do try to give it everything.' In response to their hard touring, the *Drill* EP charted at number 101, albeit for one week only. However, not long after the release, the band walked into a record store to try to buy a copy, but the agitated shop manager offered to give them one free, saying, 'We've been given a box of them to shift by the record company, and we can't get rid of them, not even for 99p.'

Realising that having their managers also as producers was probably stifling their muse, Radiohead decided on a change for the next release. The Boston-based production duo of Sean Slade and Paul Q. Kolderie, who were visiting England specifically to scout for new bands, were introduced to them. This renowned partnership had already made an indelible mark on alternative music with their accomplished production work on various albums, including Buffalo Tom's *Let Me Come Over*. By mutual agreement they were immediately pencilled in for Radiohead's next recording session.

Slade and Kolderie arranged to sit in on a rehearsal first, but were disappointed to hear that the tracks being lined up for recording, including the punk-ish 'Inside My Head' and 'Million $ Question', were inferior to the material they had heard before. Even the band seemed less than enthusiastic about the proposed tracks. Then, as Kolderie recalled in Q magazine, an exciting thing happened, 'One day in rehearsal, they burst into this other song, which I guess they had just written. When they finished it, Thom mumbles something like, "That's our Scott Walker song" . . . except I thought he said, "That's *a* Scott Walker song." Now I was pretty familiar with Scott Walker, but Jeez, there's a lot of albums and I could have missed something! We walked out of the rehearsal that night and Sean said, "Too bad their best song is a cover."' But the song wasn't a cover – it was a new composition called 'Creep'.

'At the end [of the take] everyone in the place was silent for a moment then they burst into applause. I'd never had that happen before.'

Kolderie and Slade said nothing of their feelings. In the meantime, the sessions began but did not progress well – the band seemed indifferent and the music was just not working. As a fillip to their down-hearted spirits, Kolderie suggested they plough through 'that Scott Walker song', which they seemed so enthusiastic about playing. Kolderie continued, 'At the end [of the take] everyone in the place was silent for a moment then they burst into applause. I'd never had that happen before.' Kolderie was so pleased with it he called Wozencroft who drove down to Oxford to listen. He, in contrast, remained unconvinced, asking them to work on it some more. After a few vain attempts, the band stuck with the original version. While they had been recording the track, Jonny had grumbled about it being too weak, twee and inferior. Thus when the chorus was approaching he crunched his guitar into two abrasive chords to try to ruin the take. The band carried on, it sounded fantastic and Jonny had inadvertently created the song's highlight. They had also just recorded their next single.

'I'm a creep, I'm a weirdo, what the hell am I doing here?'

Released in September, 'Creep' was an anthem of self-loathing, focussed around a man's eight month obsession with an unrequited love – 'when you were here before, couldn't look you in the eye/you're just like an angel, your skin makes me cry'. Apparently about a girl for whom Thom had 'a really really serious obsession' who used to frequent the trendy bars and cafes on Little Clarendon Street in Oxford, it reflected Thom's failure with this lady as well as his isolation from this clique – 'I'm a creep, I'm a weirdo, what the hell am I doing here?'. He was more at home with the Jericho Tavern crowd, and knew this girl would always be out of reach.

The other tracks on the *Creep* EP were less powerful. 'Lurgee' was pleasant, but much softer, even perhaps soft rock, and although it was less cluttered it was also cornier. Thom was being more positive on this track, feeling better and stronger for the end of a relationship – 'I feel better, I feel better now you've gone/I got better, I got better, I got strong'. It was supposedly a companion track to 'Creep' about 'getting rid of someone who'd been hanging around for ages and fucking you up.' Seemingly content to bite the hand that feeds him, he railed against the cheque-book waving major label on 'Inside My Head', which also deals with the quandary of leaving the 'real' world and becoming a professional pop star: '[It's] about leaving a job, and doing probably one of the strangest things you ever could do. I mean, I still find it strange to walk down the street in the middle of the day and think "Hey, I don't have to do anything until the evening!" . . . It's also about getting in a car and ramming the shop where I used to work. I just wanted to do that so badly.'

On the UK tour to promote the record, Radiohead won several positive reviews. Take this one from *Melody Maker*: 'Tonight, they are absolutely fair dinkums. Thom E. Yorke, every bit the budding, flouncing, posturing rock star . . . manages to cruise from Scott Walker to Russell Mael and back within one line . . . this Wednesday, Radiohead are the most impressive pop group in the whole wired world. Tune in, turn on, no doubt.' However, during yet more dates over Christmas, they won one of their first vicious music press reviews, when the *NME* laid into the band for a headline London show. Deliberately using some highly unflattering pictures of Thom, the caption read 'UGLEE – OH YEAH!' and launched a biting attack on Radiohead's failings, ending with the damning (although rather humorous) epitaph 'Radiohead are a pitiful, lily-livered excuse for a rock 'n' roll group.' From here on in, Radiohead's relationship with the music press was never more than civil.

Despite the strength of the lead track and the band's prolific touring, the *Creep* EP sold a meagre 6,000 copies on its release and entered at a disappointing number 78 and rose no higher. A smattering of decent reviews was overshadowed by a wall of uninterest from most magazines, currently caught up in the rocketing phenomenon of grunge. Optimistic plans for Radiohead's *Top of the Pops* debut were shelved, but in retrospect, both the band and the management recognised that progress had still been made. Hufford later told *Q* magazine, 'Bryce and I have always tried to be realistic. We hoped, as you do, that "Creep" would be a bigger hit, but at the same time it fitted in with our concept of where to be at the moment. A giant leap isn't actually healthy for a band, it needs to grow and understand naturally how things work.' Instead, Radiohead found themselves supporting the fleetingly successful Frank and Walters on a tour of yet more toilet venues around the UK in yet another rusty Transit van. Undeterred by this disappointment, Radiohead remained buoyant about their hopes and that song in particular, 'That song will always be there, and in five, six, ten years time, people will be saying that "Creep" is a fucking classic record. We know that.' Thom was right, but it wouldn't take five years.

One incident that occurred around this time is a good indication of Radiohead's unusually conservative nature. It happened at the EMI conference in September 1992, where they performed for the massed ranks of their record company, along with various other new signings, including Kingmaker. Speeches and marketing reports bored the executives during the day, while the bands they were plugging played at night. Radiohead's future marketing executive, Carol Baxter bumped into Thom and Colin for the first time at this conference, sitting quietly in a corridor. 'I thought they were junkies,' she later told *Q*, 'Bloody druggies sitting there in the corridor looking so pale. I asked Thom if he was all right. He said he was. So I asked if they wanted a drink and all they wanted was a glass of Coca-Cola. I bought that for them and we got talking.'

< c h a p t e r : 4 >

GETTING ON BETTER WITH YOUR ASSOCIATE EMPLOYEE CONTEMPORARIES

'We're going to save pop music? Nah, look at us, we're a "lily-livered excuse for a rock band". We might as well accept the truth and carry on.'
Thom

NEXT up for Radiohead was a new single, 'Anyone Can Play Guitar'. A frequent live set opener, the weirdly structured song scorned the whole concept of pop stars, reiterating Thom's uncertainty as to whether the art form he was part of is viable or is just a quagmire of self-important losers – 'I wanna be in a band when I get to heaven/anyone can play guitar'. With Thom sarcastically mocking the wannabe mentality with the line 'I wanna be, wanna be, wanna be Jim Morrison', it was another example of Radiohead's cynicism towards the industry. Musically it was rather underwhelming, with bass-and vocal-led verses leading into rather elementary choruses, which one critic rightly highlighted as oddly reminiscent of Carter USM's hit 'Do-Re-Mi' the year before. The influence of Sonic Youth and Moonshake were talked about, but were barely visible. Also, the squalling guitars were a little too close to U2's The Edge, and the vocals did little to portray Thom's ability. Overall the single was rather tame. Coming after the brilliant 'Creep', this was inevitably something of a let down, but a certain amount of airplay mixed with their continued hectic touring schedule rewarded the band with their first Top 40 hit, when 'Anyone Can Play Guitar' reached number 32.

'Am I really supposed to be excited or even challenged by Suede, for fuck's sake?'

Despite their prolific touring, there was an element of the music press who still felt that Radiohead had not 'paid their dues', that they were five privileged university lads who had barely formed the band when they were offered a mega-bucks major label deal, and that somehow this disqualified them from making quality music. In addition, Thom's increasingly vicious attacks in the media on his contemporaries made some critics feel that Radiohead were ill-qualified to be so judgemental. For example, he told *NME* , 'Am I really supposed to be excited or even challenged by Suede, for fuck's sake? I mean I don't like to be cynical, but if that is really the best that pop music can do then there's no hope for the world. There are adverts on TV that challenge me more than any song I've heard this year. There's more art in the Tango and Pot Noodle adverts than there is in 'Animal Nitrate' or anything by Bikini Kill or Cornershop.' Such outbursts did little to win him or Radiohead any friends in an already hostile environment.

Thom was convinced he knew why the press often gave them a hard time: 'It was about us being these jumped-up snots who had this deal handed to them. In all fairness, we'd only been together 2½ years and we hadn't paid any dues outside of Oxford. We became somewhat defensive and I got a reputation for being mouthy. We didn't set out to be difficult because, I swear, our major feeling at this time was bewilderment. Radiohead had to do its growing up in public.'

This fact was more apparent on the release of the band's debut album. By now, especially with the chart success of the rather average 'Anyone Can Play Guitar', the anticipation for Radiohead's debut long player was considerable. Two tracks had been recorded with Hufford and Edge at Courtyard Studios, with the remainder being completed with Kolderie and Slade, after they had impressed with their work on 'Creep'. The whole album took just three weeks to complete. The short recording time and the dual production teams meant that the record was both uneven and rushed. The sessions themselves, despite their brevity, were not trouble free: 'It was a bit of a struggle,' admitted Kolderie in *Q*. 'It was their first record and they wanted to be the Beatles . . . and they had all the ideas they'd ever come up with in twenty years of listening to records. But we managed to get it done.'

*Less than a year after being signed up, Radiohead had
established themselves as a band that refused to compromise.*

'I never had the heart to tell her [it] was about masturbation. Wanking's one of those subjects you can't really raise over Sunday dinner.'

Taking its name from a skit by the New York phone pranksters, the Jerky Boys, *Pablo Honey* had a handful of highlights. Obviously, 'Creep' was the clear peak, but there were also strong re-workings of earlier B-sides. 'You' and 'Prove Yourself' returned unexpectedly stronger than their original versions. The best re-write, however, and the album's best mellow moment was the beautiful 'Thinking About You'. It was a simple acoustic lament with Thom's powerful voice occasionally complemented by the very slightest snatches of delicate tremelo guitar, as he sings 'been thinking about you, and there's no rest/Should I still love you'. At times, Thom sounded like a more accomplished Power of Dreams, whose debut album, *Immigrants, Emigrants and Me* was almost entirely acoustic. Ironically, this gentle song was Colin's mother's favourite, which amused the singer extremely: 'I never had the heart to tell her [it] was about masturbation. Wanking's one of those subjects you can't really raise over Sunday dinner.'

Another peak was 'Stop Whispering', which again highlighted Thom's voice. The band's preference for dynamics was very visible on the intriguing 'Ripcord', and 'Lurgee', but this was where the record started to falter. The album also had its share of rubbish. 'How Do You?' was cod-punk, a cut and shut of various sub-standard punk songs, most notably Sham 69's 'The Kid's Are United', where Radiohead indulged in the kind of inane riffing and one-dimensional writing of some of the contemporaries they so readily criticised. Other tracks like 'I Can't' and 'Vegetable' were instantly forgettable, whilst tracks like 'Blow Out' were only remembered for being so poor. By the end of the record, there was a sense of anti-climax, although certain tracks could be played over and over again, and not just 'Creep' (which in itself was an accomplishment). There were hints of Sonic Youth, the Pixies, and Magazine, but there were also pseudo-U2 moments, a poor man's REM and just plain crap AOR. Keeping with the current vogue for so-called 'dry' production, Radiohead followed in the footsteps of Nirvana, Suede and the Auteurs in releasing a reverb-free, arid record. So this was no soaring, triumphant debut, rather more a modest foundation, a starting point. As *Melody Maker* said, it was 'promisingly imperfect'.

One strength of the album that could not be denied was Thom's voice and, at times, his lyrics. He himself admitted that the early critical brickbats had damaged his confidence and that he wrote much of the album with one eye on what the papers would say. Already he was being held up as the next in a long line of neurotic lyricists, of whom the Smiths had been the archetypal British act. Since them, there seemed to have been a reluctance on the part of British acts to follow in the tradition, perhaps in fear of failing against such a mighty precedent. While America exported the angst of grunge meisters like Cobain,

Love, Vedder, and Kristin Hersch, until now there had been little from Britian to answer them. Then, in 1993, there was suddenly a rash of home-grown artists who seemed to spew confessional anxiety. PJ Harvey single-handedly re-introduced the classic female singer/songwriter genre, while Richey Edwards of the Manic Street Preachers was writing material that would justifiably see him hailed as one of the lyricists of his generation. Similarly, although not as angst ridden, Brett Andersen of Suede was bringing lyrics again to the fore after a very barren spell during the aimless Madchester and late-80s indie rock eras.

'A lot of our songs – the good ones, anyway – come from crisis points in my life. Songwriting, for me, is therapy.'

Thom slotted into this new generation effortlessly as the latest member of 'neurotics anonymous'. 'Creep' was thrown at him ceaselessly as proof of his qualifications as the new misery man. The Throwing Muses and Buffalo Tom had both been produced by Kolderie and Slade, so there may have been a connection there, but in reality, Thom's lyrics were very much his own domain. Thom acknowledged this part of his muse: 'A lot of our songs – the good ones, anyway – come from crisis points in my life. Songwriting, for me, is therapy.' Some said his traumatised lyrics were little more than a cynical ploy to ensnare the listener into his world of neurosis and hang-ups and therefore shift more product – an unjust and in itself grossly cynical accusation. Those who had spent time with Thom knew that this was not the case.

Indeed, Thom already showed signs that he was not willing to accept the mantle of iconic miserabalist, as this extract from an interview in *Melody Maker* shows: 'There's always self-destruction in music. It's a matter of how you deal with it – whether you do it creatively, or just for the sake of it, like Jim Morrison. Why in his position should he be that irresponsible? I mean, there's all these sad bastards who will grow their hair long and take copious amounts of drugs because it's what someone else does – and probably that someone can handle it, and they can't. But I think a lot of great music comes from people having a really big ego and also a really big negative ego – really hating themselves. A lot of people are in bands for the weirdest reasons. Which is fair enough, it's up to them- but I don't see why I should have to listen to it!'

The media's response to *Pablo Honey* was understandably muted. They pointed out the album's weak points, and acknowledged its highlights, but generally were too busy hailing the merits of the newly arrived 'best New Band in Britain', Suede, and other lesser acts like the Auteurs and Kinky Machine. At this time, when more image-conscious bands were making an impact, the almost 'image-less' Radiohead were frequently chided for their apparent total absence of any photogenic qualities. All of this did not help their first album. Some said that in light of the mediocre debut, Radiohead were probably just a quality singles band. Indeed, Radiohead soon knew themselves that *Pablo Honey* would always be little more than a starting point, as Chris Hufford pointed out in *Mojo*, 'The band have never been happy with it, but it was a snapshot of them developing. Anyhow, first albums are usually rough around the edges, because that's what people want.' The public agreed, sending *Pablo Honey* in at number 25 in the charts, a fair beginning.

As the band seemed to be almost constantly on the road, the start of their album tour in February 1993 passed almost unnoticed. Over the course of the next two years, and with a certain unexpected turn of events, the band would go on to play a mammoth 350 dates in support of this record. Their touring commitments were increased when they released the next single, 'Pop Is Dead' in April 1993. Thom had written the song as an epitaph to 1992, a year when he felt pop music lost its way, and the vitriolic song railed against the very culture and career he was now pursuing – 'so what pop is dead/it's no great loss, so many facelifts, its face flew off'. Usually played at the end of their live set, the song was also often dedicated to Freddie Mercury (he occasionally dedicated it to the press also). 'What I was thinking about when I wrote 'Pop Is Dead' is that pop music has a very marginal part to play in pop culture.'

Unfortunately, the single was too weak to be taken seriously. The lyrics were rather puerile and the sentiment rather clichéd. The critics, ever at the ready to bring the upstart university boys down a few pegs, were harsh, justifiably so this time. Take this review in *Melody Maker:* 'Lyrical genii Radiohead are not. I was too convulsed by laughter to be able to listen further. Doubtless my elder colleagues would have it that Radiohead can "write" "songs". If this is what's known as "songwriting" give me fucking incompetent incontinent musical illiterates any day. I had previously gotten Radiohead pinned down as the indie U2 but even that comparison's too grand for them. They're the indie Kingmaker.' The public seemed to concur – 'Pop Is Dead' failed to reach the Top 40, stalling at a disappointing number 42. In defence, Thom came out with some of his most outspoken and entertaining interviews yet for the single. His habit of lambasting his contemporaries was now extended to usually sacred rock legends: 'Jim Morrison was a bimbo. He was great looking and stuff, and took loads of drugs and girls loved him, but his poetry just fucking sucked. The day they bought out a book of his poetry it was all over. It's not art, it's pop music.' He went on to say, 'I want to be in band when I get to heaven. It's the best thing you can possibly do with your life, [but] I'm not trying to define rock 'n' roll. To me, rock 'n' roll just reminds me of people with personal hygiene problems who still like getting blowjobs off complete strangers.' Nowadays, the band feel it is one of their worst songs, and never even considered putting it on the album.

One lowspot of this period was the band's cancellation of their first ever Reading Festival show. After a great secret warm-up gig at the New Cross Venue in south-east London (where their performance of 'Creep' was videoed for use as the single's future promo clip), events took a turn for the worse. Thom had been feeling unwell, and by the morning of the Reading show he could barely talk, suffering a severe bout of laryngitis. His girlfriend had to phone the management and record company to inform them he would not be able to sing that day. The slot was cancelled (and eventually went to a rather unprepared Eat, leaving Blur to steal the plaudits as they prepared to go mainstream with their forthcoming *Parklife* album). Unfortunately, many observers were less than charitable about Radiohead's last minute withdrawal. In light of Thom's self-deprecating and at times self-loathing lyrics, and his increasingly fragile media persona, critics claimed the slot was cancelled because he couldn't handle the pressure, that he was scared and that he had bottled out. He hadn't, but the episode proved to be an annoying glitch in an otherwise positive year.

> **Interviewer:** *'Did the girl ever get to hear "Creep" to the end?'*
> **Thom:** *'I got into a lot of trouble over that – I shouldn't have admitted to her being a real person. I'm sure she didn't give a shit really. She never gave a shit. She wasn't even that nice really.'*

While the band were busy touring *Pablo Honey*, a strange chain of events had started, in Israel of all places. 'Creep' had enjoyed enormous popularity on the regional radio stations over there, and before long it had become a major hit. This wave of support for the loser anthem then started to trickle through into America. The acorn for the Stateside reaction was San Francisco's Live 105 Radio. One of the DJs there had found a copy of 'Creep' on import and played it a few times on his show. An astounding phone-in response followed, forcing him to place the single on immediate heavy rotation. The news of this development spread quickly around the highly competitive and high-profile West-Coast radio circuit – a string of Californian stations, including the massively influential KROQ, that had historically been more than helpful to many British acts, including Duran Duran and Depeche Mode. Thus, within a few days 'Creep' found itself being aired across the whole of the West Coast on a daily basis. After only one week, it was KROQ's second most requested song.

Radiohead's American record company, Capitol, were not slow to realise the potential in these rumblings. With the single's heavy sales in Israel and a degree of similar success in South-East Asia, a momentum was building up that could have enormous potential. After several meetings, Capitol decided to back the single in a big way. Radiohead were shipped over to America to start a series of dates and promotional stints that were to seem be never-ending. When the group arrived at the Capitol building in Los Angeles, all of the employees were wearing Radiohead T-shirts. Within hours of landing, the band were thrown into a fearsome promotional schedule. Even their UK marketing executive, Carol Baxter, was horrified by the amount of work they were forced to do, as she told Q: '8am – breakfast with this executive, 1pm – lunch with 55 retailers, solid press interviews between, 7 pm – dinner with this many journalists and, by the way can you do a live radio phone-in a 2am? It was a 16–18 hour day with no breaks. I couldn't handle that. But they managed it. I was sitting there going grey thinking, "I'll never make my bands do this again."' Mixed with scores of live dates and continued heavy airplay across the nation, the campaign seemed to be working. Then they had an even bigger break – MTV picked up on the 'Creep' video, and placed it on immediate heavy rotation. Radiohead went skyward.

'The thing is we desperately want to be successful over here. If it was a choice between the two [UK or America] then I think I'd want success here personally.'

'Creep' arrived at a time when 'slacker' culture was everywhere. Beck was the misfit 'Loser' of his song, and Nirvana's music had been long since hijacked by a mass media anxious to jump on the latest craze, christening it grunge and even clothing catwalk models in designer versions of the slacker's wardrobe. Sub Pop, Eddie, Kurt, Courtney and Seattle were the words on everybody's lips. Thom's anthem of self-loathing struck a chord with the new generation of insecure youth, and they screamed the lyrics with proud abandon. One writer called 'Creep' 'the slacker's "Stairway To Heaven"'.

Radiohead began a series of tours that would last almost two years and would nearly destroy the band. At the beginning, however, the sheer scale of 'Creep's success was so overwhelming that they were willing participants in the

games they were asked to play. They seemed initially to want to become the all-American rock band that people thought they were. Colin told one writer 'The thing is we desperately want to be successful over here. If it was a choice between the two [UK or America] then I think I'd want success here personally.' They dressed in tight trousers, and accepted fashion magazine photo shoot assignments, including one for Iceberg Jeans. At one of these, Thom even donned hair extensions which were ludicrously tagged on to his shock of orange hair. 'I was rock,' Thom later told the press. 'There were so many elements to that period, but the hair was the worst. It was such a weird trip anyway, because suddenly we were seen as this big investment and there was money being thrown at us.'

'All these gorgeous, bikini-ed girls shaking their mammary glands, and we're playing 'Creep' and looking terrible.'

Another regrettable excursion was playing the MTV *Beach House Party*, miming to a rendition of 'Creep' and 'Anyone Can Play Guitar', both of which had to be played several times over to give the editors enough camera angles. On reflection it seemed an highly inappropriate scenario for their anthem of inadequacy, and one that the band were almost immediately embarrassed by – 'At least we played well, but I don't think the irony was lost on people. All these gorgeous, bikini-ed girls shaking their mammary glands, and we're playing 'Creep' and looking terrible.' At one point during the filming, Thom jumped into the pool, much to the horror of the MTV production crew, who desperately fished him out before he electrocuted everybody.

In Los Angeles, back at KROQ, the band reluctantly agreed to appear on a problem-page phone-in, but were taken aback by the severity of some listeners' problems. Ed did little to relieve the awkwardness when he announced that if he fell in love with a 14-year-old girl and if he thought she was mature enough, then he would sleep with her (the show's resident doctor going apoplectic upon hearing this). They even recorded a jingle for another radio station using the lyrics of 'Creep', after the DJ insinuated they weren't singing on the original. Tabloid newspapers featured the song in their pop columns with headlines screaming 'Unknown Brits take pop world by storm'. They played 'Creep' on the

Arsenio Hall show, a chain of hypermarkets included it on its muzak playlist, and they had knickers thrown on stage by the dozen in Detroit. Capitol started to run a series of 'I'm a Creep' competitions. Arnold Schwarzennegger said he wanted it included in his next film and Jon Bon Jovi allegedly said he wished he had written it. Meanwhile, *Pablo Honey* was racing up the Billboard album charts, and 'Creep' entered the singles chart at an impressive number 32. The debut album eventually went on to sell over two million copies worldwide, selling fifteen times more in the USA than the UK's press darlings Suede on their ill-fated US campaign.

Thom tried to assert some degree of integrity during this increasingly surreal circus show. To the accusations that he was hypocritical to release songs like 'Pop Is Dead' and then promote his band the way he was now doing, he said in defence, 'First of all, if you're a band on a major label coming to America, you can't help but step into *Spinal Tap* the moment you get off the plane! There was a white stretch limo waiting for us with a bar inside it. But that's just the paraphernalia of pop culture. It exists for film actors, ballet dancers and half the population of California.' Unfortunately, 'Creep' had such a head of steam that the band's growing disquiet was squashed under its own success. Just before they had headed out to tour the US, the members of Blur had offered to take them out for a drink. They later found out it was in an effort to warn them of their own hideous experiences in America. Radiohead were already regretting not having gone out for that drink.

A spate of covers of 'Creep' further reinforced the song's notoriety and cornered the band even more. Alanis Morissette took to performing the song on her tour (she has also covered Supergrass's 'Lenny'). That was understandable, but then a whole host of disparate stars started covering 'Creep' as well – Chrissie Hynde had a bash, as did former Take That teeny bop star Mark Owen ('it's terrible, really'), Rapper Chino XL eventually did a version and Frank Bennett, the kitsch Australian crooner, recorded it with his big band. Tears For Fears also played a live version, which Radiohead cringed at during a support slot to that band's *Elemental* tour in Las Vegas.'

That summer, 'Creep' blasted out of every American radio, replacing Beck's 'Loser' as the latest anthem of misery. As with Blind Melon and their 'bee girl' video, kids were walking into record stores asking for 'that creep band' or 'the record by that creep guy', not having a clue what the name of the band was, nor knowing any of their other records. At the gigs , if 'Creep' was played early, the hall would virtually empty when it finished. At one gig, a kid was spotted with a hand-painted T-shirt with the word 'Creep' scrawled on his back, underneath an arrow pointing at his head. Hufford and Bryce watched with increasing dread as the situation started to crystallise – Radiohead were on the very edge of becoming a 'flash in the pan'. After one show, a local review headline confirmed their fears: 'Say goodbye to the latest one-hit wonder.'

While 'Pop Is Dead' was grazing the Top 40 back in the UK, Radiohead were playing to sell-out gigs in America and Canada. The band had initially enjoyed the idea of the tour because it got them away from the intense pressure of the UK music scene, and the criticisms that were being heaped on them by their native press. However, within a few weeks, things had turned sour on the road as well. With a re-issued 'Creep' hitting the number 7 spot in the UK (their first Top 10) in September 1993, the gruelling slog continued. Parlophone sent the band a bottle of expensive champagne as a celebration, but they were too busy rehearsing to notice. The over-emphasis on 'Creep' was also happening in the UK as well. The band played one show in Canterbury where the crowd kept shouting for 'Creep' even after they had played it, so the demoralised band rendered an acoustic version as well as several other normal ones. Their other songs were largely ignored.

In Australia their experience was particularly humiliating. Playing a record that no-one really knew, Radiohead performed to half-empty halls night after night. Then the news filtered through that 'Creep' had become a hit in France, where after an initial flop it had been resurrected by its inclusion in the soundtrack for the film *Cyclo*. The success just seemed like it would never end, but with each new breakthrough, Radiohead's hearts dropped a little further. The song even sold 152 copies in Poland, where it was released by a record label who had formerly been run by the Boy Scouts movement. In Bangkok, a moment of irony at least made the band laugh. They walked into a bar for a drink and a break from the onslaught, only to find the resident band covering 'Creep'. They listened in resigned silence, but enjoyed it and after the band had finished clapped raucously. The band looked on bewildered, totally unaware who their audience was.

To add to their considerable reservations about the over-emphasis being placed on 'Creep', Radiohead had been writing new material, far, far superior to their first batch of songs, but were unable to play or record any of it. They were playing songs they hated to audiences who didn't want to listen (other than for 'Creep') and they wanted out, but they couldn't. They spent the summer playing scores of festivals, followed by yet another American tour, this time supporting

Belly, and then turned down an arena tour with label-mates Duran Duran because they were simply exhausted.

The band were then packed off on a European tour to see out the year supporting James, but the atmosphere was degenerating. At Hamburg they called an emergency meeting to air their problems, and this did appear to paper over some of the cracks – the performance that night was their best for several months. Still, for Radiohead there was an unusually large amount of drinking after shows and the atmosphere was very tense – no-one was really talking to anyone else in the band and they would each go their separate ways after a gig.

'We joined this band to write songs and be musicians, but we spent a year being jukeboxes instead.'

Looking back, the low point had arrived after the Belly tour, when the band were so demoralised and argumentative that they even considered splitting up. 'Creep' had turned into a monstrous albatross, a millstone around their necks that threatened to destroy them. Worse still, if they did manage to carry on, the song's enormous success had the potential to overshadow anything they might ever record in the future. Already the media were suggesting that Radiohead's future might not be too rosy: 'Just how are they going to top the emotion of 'Creep'?' wrote *Raygun*. 'How are they going to create a solid body of work after writing one soul-searing classic? Maybe like Nirvana did with "Teen Spirit", they should leave "Creep" behind them. Maybe even take it out of their live sets. But, that would be stretching it.'

Radiohead were not enjoying their success – they hadn't for a long time. Although *Pablo Honey* sold in the millions, they knew it was because of a successful single, not because it was a successful album. All that the 'Creep' fiasco had done was line their pockets (Thom bought 'the house that Creep built' with his royalties) and prevent them from writing or recording their new material. 'We joined this band to write songs and be musicians,' Jonny told *Q* magazine, 'but we spent a year being jukeboxes instead. We felt in a creative stasis because we couldn't release anything new.' For a while, Thom rechristened the song 'Crap'. He could be vicious about the whole episode: 'We sucked

Satan's cock. It took a year-and-a-half to get back to the people we were . . . to cope with it emotionally.'

By late 1993, Radiohead were reeling from the enormous experience they had gone through. With the band still exhausted, still arguing and yet fortunately still together, a more removed Thom Yorke was able to reflect with a little more objectivity about their scrape with fleeting fame. He admitted he had lost perspective completely, and that he was convinced he could go solo, as he told *NME*, 'As soon as you get any success you disappear up your own arse and lose it forever. When I got back to Oxford I was unbearable. You start to believe you're this sensitive artist who has to be alone . . . this melodramatic, tortured person, in order to create wonderful music. The absolute opposite is true. All those things happen to you anyway, you don't have to sit there and make them happen. Otherwise you're a human being.'

Manager Chris Hufford continued: 'Thom found it particularly hard, because all the attention was on him. That whole dilemma of the commercial success against artistic integrity. It was hard for him to find where he sat in that whole framework. Who he was, what he was.' The other members of Radiohead were all showing scars as well. Jonny had become much more introverted, lying on his bunk alone at the back of the tour bus engrossed in his collection of BBC audio books. He didn't speak for hours and would then intersperse his limited conversation with quotes from his favourite Sherlock Holmes audio novel. As one observer put it, 'A few more months of this and he'll be royally mad.' Ed had bought a cottage but otherwise kept himself to himself. Colin seemed to identify with the road crew more and spent many nights getting drunk with them, avoiding having much contact with the rest of the band. Even Phil, normally so laid back and grounded (his sarcastic nickname is Mad Dog Selway), seemed out of sorts, choosing to concentrate on phoning his fiancée and arranging his forthcoming nuptials.

For two years, they had toured a record that was effectively finished after only six months. Now they were paying the price. 'Creep' had taken on a life of its own and the band nearly split up because of that, although Colin later said 'It was more of a breakdown than a breakup.' They had to regroup and start work on their second album. Unfortunately, despite being back at home, rested and excited about their new material, Radiohead's life did not get any easier. If anything, the creative stresses only got worse.

< chapter: 5 >

I DON'T WANT TO BE KRIPPLED

RADIOHEAD opened 1994 by rehearsing new material at a converted fruit farm building in a remote part of Oxfordshire. They had acquired the barn with royalties from the sales of 'Creep', and were hoping to use the song's own earnings to shake off its debilitating legacy of that very same song. They then booked into RAK Studios in north-west London, to begin work with the second album's chosen producer, John Leckie. Although Kolderie and Slade were still in touch with the band, it was Leckie who got the nod for the album. One of the most famous producers in the world, Leckie had initially started as an engineer at Abbey Road Studios, before working with Pink Floyd, the Fall, Simple Minds, Ride and the Verve. He had also been at the helm for much of the protracted Monmouth Studios sessions for the Stone Roses' painfully delayed, and ultimately ill-fated second album, *The Second Coming*. Radiohead were mainly attracted to his work because of his production credits with both Magazine and XTC, and Andy Partridge of XTC's psychedelic spin-off band, the Dukes of Stratosphear. Radiohead sent him a copy of *Pablo Honey* during the middle of 1993, and he wasn't particularly enamoured, but when he received a demo of rough songs for their next project, he was far more interested. So, after an initial delay while he finished a lengthy project with Ride for their *Carnival Of Light* album, Leckie joined Radiohead at RAK. 'Even at this early stage the signs were good. Everyone knew that there would be some big songs on the record because good demos had been done of them – the guitars and the singing and the ideas were there. One thing I think that's important with Radiohead songs is to get the feel right.'

They began work together on the last day of February 1994. Radiohead requested Studio 1 which was regularly bathed in a natural light. Unfortunately, things almost immediately started to turn sour. At this early stage, all the band had was a demo version of 'High And Dry' which no-one liked, and a very basic version of 'Nice Dream' (which had different lyrics to the final version and can be heard on the compilation album *Volume 13*). Apart from that, it was a blank piece of paper waiting to be filled. Parlophone pencilled an autumn 1994 release and began to pressurise the band for the first single. Although there had been other singles since 'Creep', there was a pervading desire for a strong follow-up, especially if they were to build on their popularity in America. This pressure proved crippling. Attempting to give them what they wanted, the band and Leckie recorded the rudiments of four tunes, all of which might have worked as the next single: 'The Bends', 'Sulk', 'Killer Cars' and 'Nice Dream'. Every couple of days, the management and record company would call in to the studio to listen, and after each visit they left with increasingly furrowed brows, as all Radiohead could produce were a few interesting drum sounds. Something appeared to be going horribly wrong. The four attempted tracks were just too busy, too cluttered. At one point, a record company executive listened to what they had recorded so far and raged, 'Look, I don't intend to take some fucking prog rock album. What the fuck is going on?'

'It's a brilliant thing to have a big hit, but it's a sodding nightmare because you have to follow it up with something just as good.'

At this stage, the stasis was frustrating the band, but its repercussions on the management were more serious. The American record company Capitol were holding back on their option for the second album until they had heard some decent new material. Meanwhile, Hufford and Edge were getting increasingly nervous. Hufford recalled to *Q* magazine: 'I was shitting myself to be honest, me and my partner started shopping around for another group to manage because they really didn't look like they'd make it. I'm glad they proved us wrong.' In the meantime, he signed a management contract with Supergrass, so his time had clearly not been wasted.

'It was horrible but I think that's the problem with a university education. You just end up thinking too much.'

The escalating tension and pressure on the band inevitably infected their morale. With them still exhausted from the previous year, and with friction growing apparently unchecked, the situation began to disintegrate. The recordings were fraught with misunderstandings, as the five school friends no longer seemed able to communicate. Hufford blames himself for many of these difficulties: 'Looking back, a lot of it was paranoia. It was a fear of actually recording anything. It's a brilliant thing to have a big hit, but it's a sodding nightmare because you have to follow it up with something just as good. Radiohead are infuriating sometimes, because they hate anything that's second best. They felt a lot of pressure; but most of the problems were in their heads . . . We didn't understand the pressure Thom was under. We attempted to [push for an autumn release] for the right reasons, but we fucked up majorly. We weren't as considerate as we should have been.' Everyone knew it was going wrong, as Ed explained in *Spin*, 'It was horrible, at one stage everyone was trying to find their get-out clauses. The worst thing was that our friendship was being altered simply because we were questioning everything too much, questioning the fundamentals of what we were doing. It was horrible but I think that's the problem with a university education. You just end up thinking too much.'

Leckie watched all this and gradually began to work out what was happening. Two months had gone by with very little progress to speak of. His years of experience told him that he had to do something fast, so he ordered the whole band, apart from Thom, to leave the studio for a few days. With the singer now completely isolated, Leckie told him to play the songs he had ready on an acoustic guitar only. Thom relished this lack of restraint: 'The thing John Leckie used to say all the time was, "Do what the fuck you like," and nobody had ever said it before in that way. It was like being at art college: in the first year they said, "You can do whatever you want" . . . I just needed something to start me off.' Realising they had pushed their charges too hard, the management and record company relented and stopped demanding the next single. The pressure was lifted still further. Radiohead began to turn the corner.

However, things were still a little fragile when the rest of the band rejoined Thom. A forthcoming world tour had already been booked to promote the autumn release of *The Bends*, but with that prospect now virtually impossible, it was decided that Radiohead would play these lengthy dates anyway, if for no other reason than to help them gel again. Thus they played gigs in the Far East, Europe, Australasia and America, which went some way to helping the band get their perspective back. At the London Astoria show at the end of May, the signs of recovery were there, mixed with remnants of their problems. Their dislike of playing London gigs (they had always fretted that everyone would hate them) was evident immediately before the show, when things did not seem too rosy. Thom was in a terrible state, nervous about playing in front of 2,000 people, and telling *NME* that 'It's a problem because I'm fucking ill and physically I'm completely fucked and mentally I've had enough. It may be great because of that but it may be awful and it all rests on me, and I've never been in that position before, not in Britain. I don't care about anywhere else.'

Despite these doubts the show was awesome. After the rigorous schedules of the last few months, one great thing had come out of the trauma – Radiohead were a transformed band live. Their show was so much stronger, and the breadth and diversity of the new material was undeniable. And Thom's star persona, polished by months of promotional activity and gigging, had increased exponentially. The performance was so good that the band's version of 'My Iron Lung' was used in its entirety for the album cut, with a new vocal dubbed over the top (MTV even used direct footage of the song as the video). Although the band were still tense, this Astoria gig was a flickering sign that they were perhaps, finally, coming back to life.

In many ways, 'My Iron Lung' was a pivotal track for Radiohead. It had been written on the morning of the cancelled Reading Festival performance the previous year, when Thom's mangled throat had forced him to pull out. As he sat at home desperately disappointed, Thom recalled a tune that had been in his head for many months, and the words to match began to suggest themselves, a verbal casting-off of the baggage that 'Creep' had brought, the end of an era. 'It's me trying to kill the beast,' Thom told the media. 'I wrote the second half of the song when we were in America – most of it in one day. It normally takes me ages.' It was on this same tour bus with his acoustic guitar and tape recorder that Thom wrote the majority of *The Bends*. The title 'My Iron Lung' came from a picture he used to carry around of a sick child from the 1950s, cocooned inside a dehumanising monstrous iron lung – it reminded him of how 'Creep' was a monster, and yet at the same time how that song had simultaneously provided them with their very life blood. He sings 'You don't mean it but it hurts like hell.' Thom later lost the picture.

The album sessions now switched to the Manor Recording Studios in Oxfordshire, where progress continued unabated for an entire month. Appearances at Glastonbury (alongside a veritable Britpop feast of Blur, Oasis and Pulp) and a blistering gig at Reading followed. The band meanwhile headed off for summer dates in Mexico which went well on the surface, but tensions resurfaced. Although recording was going well, there were still some serious divisions that needed to be discussed. So, with admirable objectivity, Radiohead held another meeting and aired all of their reservations, frustrations and concerns. This time it was a fully cathartic and cleansing experience and it worked. As Thom told *NME*, 'It just all came out. When we started our little band, it was never really about being friends or anything. We were all playing our instruments in our bedrooms and we wanted to play them with someone else. Years and years of tension and not saying anything to each other . . . it all came out. We were spitting and fighting and crying and saying all the things that you don't want to talk about. It completely changed what we did and we all went back and did the album and it all made sense.'

'They're drug-free, as you probably know. And they do the *Guardian* crossword every day.'

Revitalised and with renewed confidence from these tour dates, Radiohead returned to the studio and completed the sessions for the second album without any further hitches. The basic acoustic tracks of Thom's were played alongside a drum and guide vocal, which despite this being an unusual way to record, seemed to work well. 'That's probably how I do most things actually,' Leckie told *Melody Maker*, 'and I don't I understand why other people don't do it like that because you've got a vocal and rhythm guitar, and most songs – if they're written on guitar – stand up like that.'

Leckie also revealed some interesting facts about Radiohead's recording habits in an article in *NME*: 'It all comes from Thom really, and they all sort of gather round and support him. It's a good chemistry because Jonny's pretty wild, you never really know what he's going to do. When they're in the studio, they jump around the same way they do on stage and knock things over, and Thom rolls on the floor just doing a guide track. It's pretty exciting.' He also told *Melody Maker*, 'They're drug-free, as you probably know. The occasional little puff or something with me . . . it's not so much that it's frowned upon, it's just something they don't connect with. And they do the *Guardian* crossword every day. That's the most important thing, I'd say. Things like that, which set them apart from the usual lads' kind of thing.'

Certain tracks proved more difficult to record than others. 'Sulk' was an awkward one for Thom – he had actually written the basis of the song when he was only sixteen, essentially about the Hungerford massacre when Michael Ryan shot sixteen villagers in the streets of a quiet English town. The actual final recording took only a weekend, but several versions had been tried previously, only to be ditched. Yet, when it was finished, neither Leckie nor the band could put their finger on why it had been such a problem. Thom changed the final line from 'Just shoot your gun', which he now deemed inappropriate in the light of Kurt Cobain's recent suicide. Strangely, the song went from being the one the record company insisted would be a hit, to the least liked track on the record. Since then, the band have only ever played it once, grudgingly, in Japan.

'High And Dry' was perhaps the most peculiar of all the tracks to be recorded. They had demo-ed it many months previously, but everyone hated it, and they dismissed it, leaving the tape to gather dust. The original version was based around a lifted Soul II Soul sample, and Phil's experiments with a new skin on his bass drum. At first, they discarded it, saying Thom sounded too much like Rod Stewart. Then, when the sessions for *The Bends* were almost over, someone dug the tape out, dusted it down and suggested they try again. It was so old that the band actually had to re-learn their own lines for the track, but eventually used the initial demo version. Ironically, when it was complete, the band said it was too good for this album and that they were going to save it for their third long player. Fortunately, someone persuaded them otherwise.

For 'Fake Plastic Trees' they used a world class cellist who works with Peter Gabriel and a student violinist who was a friend of the band. There was some trepidation about this mix of players but the result was perfect. Thom's vocal performance was inspired by a Jeff Buckley gig, after which he went to the studio and recorded the vocal line in two takes, then broke down in tears. 'Planet Telex' was recorded under the influence of several bottles of wine. The chef at RAK was off sick, so the band were sent to a restaurant with £100 to feed themselves. Drinking while recording is something that Radiohead rarely do, but in this case it proved highly fruitful. Thom recorded the vocal in one take, lying on the floor, swigging from another bottle of wine. After 'Planet Telex' Leckie moved alone into Abbey Road to start mixing. At the same time, the master tapes were also given to Kolderie and Slade, who had produced *Pablo Honey*, to see what they would mix from these sessions.

During the final stages of *The Bends*, Radiohead released their first new single for over a year, 'My Iron Lung'. It was an incredibly strong return, but their fragile morale was immediately dealt a hefty blow when BBC Radio One decided it was 'too raucous' to be playlisted, thus guaranteeing it minimal airplay exposure. Despite this, their fans propelled the record to number 23 in the charts in mid-October, no mean feat in the circumstances, but it was an undeniable disappointment. A fortnight later, Thom and Jonny performed a rapturously welcomed acoustic set in New York, before the band retired for the Yuletide period. It had been a big year.

The album had taken nearly a year to complete, and in those long months the band had looked likely to split up on more than one occasion. That grim reality had shaken them back to their core motivations for being in the band – making music with their friends. They had emerged weary, happy, still together and with a batch of songs that was quite simply astounding.

●　　●　　●

By the time Radiohead released their second album, Britain was fully in the grip of the musical phenomenon that came to be called Britpop. In 1994, there was an inspired renaissance of British music that saw a whole collection of new native bands break through. In the early nineties, against a backdrop of American slacker-driven grunge culture, British music had been largely ignored, even derided, ever since the demise of Madchester. Alongside this American rock domination, the commercial charts were swamped with one-hit wonders, cover versions, novelty songs and old timers. A brief flurry of activity around speed-fuelled, sartorially focussed pseudo-punk bands such as S*M*A*S*H, heralded the so-called 'new wave of new wave', but this had little significance other than rejuvenating an interest in live bands, thus paving the way for Britpop.

Some observers have argued that Britpop's genesis lay in Suede, led by the enigmatic Brett Andersen, whose highly stylised, romantic London dramas and peculiarly camp Englishness provided British music with the first post-indie band who steadfastly refused to be middle class, refused to churn out three-minute perfect pop songs and carried themselves with a degree of swagger. Suede's eponymously titled, award-winning debut album marked the first time for years that British music had claimed a sense of occasion, and suddenly all eyes were turned back on the UK's own rich heritage, rather than on the American record archives.

Blur were also very active in regenerating this English fascination, particularly with their 1994 classic *Parklife*, and its predecessor *Modern Life Is Rubbish*, and with their irony-drenched character-bedevilled stories of twitching net curtains and ultra-reality in modern Britain. The late-comers who then took all honours were, of course, Oasis, who were only releasing their first single at the same time as Blur's second long player, but within months they had grown into the most talked about British band for years. The volatile Gallagher brothers' fiery relationship and their yob anthem songs, mixing British working class hero status with the advent of the so-called 'new lad', sold millions of copies of their albums, with *What's The Story (Morning Glory)* repeatedly breaking records. In turn, this Britpop phenomenon launched thousands of copies of the lads' magazine *Loaded*, rejuvenated the careers of other British performers like Shaun Ryder and canonised what John Major reviled as 'the yob culture'.

'Who do you think you are kidding, Mr Cobain? Enough is enough! We don't want plaid. We want crimplene, glamour, wit and irony.'

Britpop's ranks were swelled by a host of quality bands, and also hordes of lesser acts. Supergrass hit the big time after the release of their first album *I Should Coco*, while Pulp, after an incredible fifteen years, finally broke through, whereupon Jarvis Cocker's unique style and personality were hailed as genius. Less impressive but still selling records were bands like the Boo Radleys, Shed Seven, Portishead, the Bluetones, Marion, Powder, Dodgy, and the fleetingly

fashionable but soon-to-be-forgotten Sleeper. In the process, the Modfather Paul Weller's career was revitalised, as were British fashion, design, tourism and so forth. Certain older bands became highly fashionable again, as Blur, Oasis and others constantly name-dropped their influences, like the Kinks, Steve Harley and the Cockney Rebel and, of course, the Beatles.

The British media loved it. The music press ran pieces such as *Select*'s banner headline 'Yanks Go Home' a humorous piece which included lines such as 'Who do you think you are kidding, Mr Cobain? Enough is enough! We don't want plaid. We want crimplene, glamour, wit and irony. If 1992 was the American year then it's time to bring on the home guard.' The tabloids camped outside Liam Gallagher's house, they trailed Damon and his celebrity girlfriend around Tesco, and the Groucho Club in Soho became the haunt of any self-respecting Britpop icon. The untimely demise of Kurt Cobain, the mainstream hijacking of grunge and the rise of such a plethora of talented home grown acts meant that the recent American hegemony fell before the newcomers. Record sales rocketed by 14 per cent in 1994 alone, reaching an all-time high of £1.5 billion. Cool Britannia had arrived.

'In this day and age, to hear the squeek of a finger moving up and down a guitar string, is so much more exciting than a million miles of feedback.'

It was a rich new seam of British talent, but Radiohead had absolutely nothing to do with it. During Britpop's rise in 1994, Radiohead were mostly abroad touring the dredges of the *Pablo Honey* project, or deep in studios recording its follow-up. They possessed none of the irony, the personalities, the looks nor the peculiar Britishness that most Britpop bands thrived on. While Oasis sang of cocaine and razorblades, Thom (hardly the pin-up type) filled his lyrics with angst and trauma. Blur talked of 'Boys and Girls', whilst Thom admitted he wrote 'music to listen to on holiday in Beirut'. Radiohead, and their music, just did not fit. For them, Britpop was something that happened to other people.

• • •

Further evidence of this fact came with the release of the band's second album, *The Bends*, in March 1995. But before this came the single 'High And Dry' (released as a double A-side with 'Planet Telex'), which reached number 17 in the singles chart. Although some observers claimed it was unnervingly close to U2's 'Stay (Faraway So Close)', a comparison that would dog Radiohead for some time to come, the track was justifiably a commercial success. Thom's eloquent and lilting voice was, of course, the strong point, backed here by a simple acoustic foundation, with minimalist drums and instrumentation. Sparingly produced, it was a refreshing snatch of quality songwriting of astonishing depth, as the *NME* rightly pointed out in their review, saying 'in this day and age, to hear the squeek of a finger moving up and down a guitar string, is so much more exciting than a million miles of feedback.'

' 'Fake Plastic Trees' was the one where, despite us having a tough time in the studio, it turned into a real emotional experience.'

Industry whispers that suggested Radiohead were about to release something special was confirmed on the release of the album on 13 March. Drenched in heavy emotion, acoustic refrains and peculiar, obscure yet heart-wrenching lyrics, *The Bends* was a colossal leap forward from their debut album.

The opening track, the abrasive 'Planet Telex', was oddly one of the weaker ones, but the juddering, reverb-heavy song was still immediate evidence that the band were unrecognisable from the outfit that had given us *Pablo Honey*. As Jonny told the media, 'It was an uncomfortable track from its very inception, but one that grew impressively: [when Thom was recording it] I was just watching the television, thinking "What is this?" It sounded really tedious. But then it all came together quite beautifully.' The second track was the album's first rock masterpiece – 'The Bends' – which clearly exhibited Jonny's by-now unique and arguably unparalleled guitar style and technique. Filled with odd sounds and fleeting atmospheres all wrung from his six-string, this was Jonny's song.

Then came the first of at least four ballads that could only be described as 'classic'. The single 'High And Dry' would ordinarily have been the album's highlight, but when followed by the haunting and simply beautiful 'Fake Plastic Trees' it was merely one of a number of stunners.

'Fake Plastic Trees' is a perfect example of Thom's odd lyrical and vocal style. Many of the actual words are unclear, poorly pronounced, and often apparently meaningless, such as 'a cracked polystyreneman who just crumbles and burns'. Yet somehow the emotion and feeling that he manages to extract from his voice mean that the listener finds the song highly moving. Thom claimed this was the first song where he was totally happy with his lyrics: 'When we were recording The Bends nobody looked for big emotions, which is why it worked. But 'Fake Plastic Trees' was the one where, despite us having a tough time in the studio, it turned into a real emotional experience.'

Elsewhere, the other slower tracks provided yet more highlights, with the next single 'Street Spirit (Fade Out)' and the more enigmatic 'Bullet Proof . . . I Wish I Was' proving that Radiohead were unrivalled in their mastery of melancholia and metaphor. They mixed sweet pop melodies with vitriolic lyrics and then heartfelt lyrics with caustic instrumentation, both styles joined equally seamlessly. For example, over the elegant and emotive instrumentation of 'Street Spirit' Thom sings the dark words 'cracked eggs, dead birds/scream as they fight for life/I can feel death, I can see its beady eyes'. The effect provoked over-use of the words 'epic' and 'grandeur' in the press, but the choice of words was understandable – the very scale of Radiohead's ambition and sound were enormous. At the same time, however, their sound never quite tripped into bombastic stadium rock, staying just the right side of pompous.

Other tracks were more abrasive but no less enthralling. Songs like 'My Iron Lung' and 'Sulk' were harder listening, more piercing and clattering, but repeated listening revealed they were equally compelling. Throughout there were numerous examples of Radiohead's dynamics, great crescendos of noise dying in seconds into the most gentle refrains, before building once again into ear-splitting, heart-wrenching climaxes.

Radiohead dedicated the album to the late Bill Hicks, a comedian from Austin, Texas who had recently died from cancer of the pancreas. His career was brief and cruelly under-recognised, possibly because some of his material was deemed just too offensive to some people. Hicks had lived recklessly and died young, aged only 32. The album title itself was the name of a condition that affects divers who surface too quickly, the rapid change increasing the level of nitrogen in the bloodstream, leaving them paralysed, and which can often be fatal. The medical focus which gave the album its title was prevalent throughout, with Thom's highly idiosyncratic lyrics thinly detailing his own history of physical complications. Having said that, Jonny was keen in public to steer people away from giving such a narrow interpretation to the record's themes.

The album sleeve depicts what appears to be an open-mouthed death mask but is in fact a photograph of a plastic dummy used by medical staff at the John Radcliffe Hospital in Oxford to train people in resuscitation. This was then digitally blended with a photograph of Thom himself. Thom and Dan Rickwood (whom he went to college with and who had always helped with the band's artwork) had left the artwork until they only had three days before deadline. Originally, they had wanted to use a picture of an iron lung similar to the one Thom once possessed, but they couldn't find one. They plumped for the dummy because 'even though he was made of plastic he had this expression which was somewhere between agony and ecstasy, which was just right for the record'.

For once, here was an album with barely a weak track on it, and this was reflected in the critical applause at the time of its release, which was substantial: 'a powerful, bruised and desperate record of frighteningly intensity,' said *Melody Maker*, who also claimed it was 'almost unbearably, brilliantly, physically tortured by the facts of being human', before asking 'Are Radiohead the spirit of prog-rock reborn?' *NME* was even more enthusiastic, saying, 'Make no mistakes, *The Bends* will be one of, and quite possibly *the,* indie rock album of the year.' (Radiohead got their own back on the once hostile magazine by stickering the album casing with this quote, but choosing to leave out the word 'indie'.) The group knew the album was good, so did their management and record company. But in the current Britpop climate, there were grave doubts about whether anyone would want to listen to such serious music, even after the press had hailed its launch. Only time would tell.

< chapter: 6 >

TASTES LIKE THE REAL THING

Interviewer: *'Did the "next U2" label piss you off?'*
Thom: *'No more than people saying I was going to be the next rock martyr. Actually, that was worse.'*

WITH Radiohead about to launch into a world tour to promote *The Bends*, there was much talk about them at last realising their long-talked of potential for becoming 'the next U2'. This label was a label that had dogged them ever since the US success of 'Creep', and was now being reinforced by the timeless and 'epic grandeur' of their second album. The common perception was that the Oxford band would follow in the footsteps of U2, and more recently the Cranberries, in sweeping the enormous US market. Thom was hailed as the next arena messiah. One magazine would later juxtapose images of U2 and Radiohead with the headline, 'The kings are dead . . . long live the kings.' This was not a new experience for the band – a British magazine had once called them 'the new Mott the Hoople', even though they had never heard of the seventies rock band at the time.

Radiohead had never cared much for this 'U2' tag. When it was initially suggested they felt they were hopelessly inadequate, and they knew they needed an album of more diversity and depth than their debut. Now they had this with *The Bends*, they still didn't want the burden of keeping stadium rocks dwindling flame alive. As Thom once told the press: 'One of the things with 'Creep' . . .

was that we were suddenly shot into the Top 40, and we had done very little to deserve that. It was a good song, but we didn't have any fan base, no longevity – we looked to bands like U2 and R.E.M., hard working bands who had built up a fan base and could thus sustain some longevity.' He continued, 'Elvis Costello said that America is like the Mount Everest of places to tour. Because it takes its victims, you have to work hard – really, really hard, in order to be successful in America. But once you've been successful in America, and you've taken a while to get there, it's the thing. You've really achieved something. But boy, does it take its toll on bands. Lots of bands have split up. Lots of British bands never achieve it.' Asked whether Radiohead were ripe for this challenge he replied, 'No, not really . . . we've never thought about it. There's more talk about it around us – people speculating – particularly in Britain . . . If it happens, it happens, but the only way it will happen is if we're comfortable with that . . . which we're not at the moment.'

• • •

Q: *'How is the tour coming along?'*
Thom: *'I'm here to sell pieces of plastic with a diameter of 12 inches.'*

Thom: *'It's best when we're playing when we're in a dream state. If it's a good show, you play well and feel that when you've left the stage there's something in the air that wasn't there when you started, then you've really done something.'*

Most of 1995 was spent touring *The Bends*, during which time a substantial groundswell of support gradually built up around the album. It originally reached number 6 in the UK charts, but had faired much less well than *Pablo Honey* in America. Reviews had been solidly appreciative, although not universally frenzied. However, a slew of hit singles and stunning live dates over the course of 1995 reinforced the initial acclaim, so that by December it was being hailed as the record of the year in many polls.

Before that, however, the band had a busy year touring ahead of them, starting off with a UK tour, including a homecoming show at Oxford's Apollo with the Candyskins and Supergrass. With the full impact of the brilliant second album yet to be felt, critics still often sharpened their claws whenever Radiohead took to the stage. The gig was rammed with more media and industry people than true fans, and opinions of the new live show varied wildly. While *NME* said, 'Put simply much of Radiohead's new stuff appears to be all but classic . . . they look like the most unlikely heroes imaginable,' *Melody Maker* were somewhat less charitable, saying 'Radiohead are Ugly Boy Syndrome made sound . . . they looked stultified and weary. How can a band sound this dinosaurish this early in their career?'

Unfortunately, *The Bends* met with a similarly uninterested response in America. With the public still hankering after 'Creep Mk II', the traumatic, anxious scenarios of *The Bends* was almost completely unpalatable. Capitol Records had finally taken up the option on the album after their initial reluctance, but the pressure to produce a big hit single was still there, and when 'Fake Plastic Trees' was released in the US, the band were asked to record a 'radio mix' that would be more suitable to conservative American airwaves. Of course, Radiohead refused, with the result that the single received very little airplay and charted poorly. Bizarrely, one gimmick that was allowed was a give-away of condoms to fans, in association with the radio station WXRK. The free condom packets had the station's logo on one side, with *The Bends* artwork on the reverse, with the words 'Our listeners come first.' Despite this, and the forthcoming dates across the continent, *The Bends* was effectively a flop in America.

The US leg of the world tour started in early March in Los Angeles – between now and the start of the next album recording sessions, Radiohead would tour the US no less than five times. Ed told *Q* how they were undeterred by this early disappointment: 'Because they became so huge in Britain very quickly, bands like Happy Mondays and Stone Roses came back to America with completely the wrong attitude. You have to keep touring.' Jonny agreed: 'There are lots of double standards with British bands when they talk about America. They like to talk boldy about it, yet they want to conquer it. We're in awe of America.'

> '*What REM gave us was a sense that you can be as emotional as you like in what you do. That's what it's about. It was extraordinarily good therapy.*' **Thom**

Radiohead's best opportunity to play to the massed American public came in the summer of 1995 as support slot for REM, currently promoting their *Monster* album in Europe and the USA. As they were one of Radiohead's biggest influences, the offer from the Athens, Georgia band came as a pleasant shock and a fantastic chance to meet yet more of their heroes. (Thom had already met Elvis Costello, and claimed not to have slept for six months afterwards.) Michael Stipe had been watching MTV at home when he saw the video for 'Fake Plastic Trees' – he went out and bought *The Bends*, listened to it and then called his management straightaway to book Radiohead as support. Speaking to *Raygun* about REM, Ed said 'They're great songs to cover. They are very easy to play. We used to do "Losing My Religion" and "Life's Rich Pageant."' We like music that moves people. We like bands that have an element of melancholy in their music. Unfortunately, this element tends to get lost in most pop or rock music.' Colin even remembered listening to *Reckoning* on his Walkman on the way to his school exams!

A girl walked up past Michael Stipe over to Thom's seat, where she asked him for his autograph.

The first show was at the Milton Keynes Bowl along with Blur and the Cranberries, before some European dates and then the American leg, which started on 8 September in Miami. That first US gig alone grossed gate receipts of over $450,000. If Radiohead had ever wanted to taste arena rock, big style, then this was their chance. For Thom, the experience was pivotal, and he struck up a friendship with Michael Stipe that taught him much about life as a pop icon. He would watch in bemusement as Stipe played the corporate game, switching from media icon and bankable commodity to personable friend with consumate ease. As he watched Thom listened and learned, with a not inconsiderable amount of wisdom bestowed from Stipe himself over many a bottle of beer. Ironically, one of the tour's most memorable occasions came as Radiohead and REM were eating in a restaurant, and a girl walked up past Michael Stipe over to Thom's seat, where she asked him for his autograph. Thom later described this as 'one of the most embarrassing moments of my life . . . I hid my face in a napkin for 5 minutes.'

The entire summer was filled with moments like these for Thom and Radiohead. Mike Mills told them not to wear anything they ever wanted to keep in case they

When Radiohead supported REM, Thom struck up a friendship with Michael Stipe.

were mobbed. He also read out a letter from President Clinton sympathising with him for his recent stomach illness. Stipe spent many hours drinking with Thom and revealing indirectly how he had coped with becoming a phenomenon, integrity intact. They emphasised the importance of continuing to write music and enjoying the process, in spite of the circus around them. When the members of Radiohead were nervous one night before playing to 50,000 people, Stipe told them, 'Get nervous when you realise you can do it. When you can go through a whole evening having talked to 50 people and not remember a fucking word of any of it. Then you really are in trouble.' Then he walked on stage and spoke the now-oft-quoted compliment, 'Radiohead are so good it scares me.'

'That whole idea of being Thom Yorke, "the personality" . . . I don't want to die having been just that.'

At many of the US gigs, the front seats were reserved for corporate ticket holders, while the moshing fans were kept way back at the far end of the auditorium. Radiohead's 30-minute slot each night presented none of the pressures of headlining, despite the size of the crowds. They interspersed these shows with their own headline tour, which would average around 800 people a night, rather than 50,000, and found that the skills involved in playing each show equally well were very demanding.

REM played numerous pranks on Radiohead, who were actually *enjoying* themselves most of the time. Michael Stipe would often drive a remote control car around the stage to try to distract Thom and Jonny. At the end of the tour, Radiohead therefore planned to invade the stage as REM played their last song, but the tour manager forbade them, so instead they simply put a note on Stipe's mike stand, complete with a smiley face cartoon, saying, 'Thanks for having us, you've been brilliant – Radiohead.' Thom was unequivocally gushing about their experience: 'We talked about it as a sort of fantasy two years ago. It stayed fairly unreal, right up until the end of the last show.'

Despite these experiences, the band still had their reservations about their new roles, but now seemed far better equipped to cope – take this quote from Thom in *Vox*: 'Michael Stipe's a lovely bloke, and he's coped with fame very well – which helps me, 'cos I find myself having to fight certain aspects of it at the moment. I don't like my old friends talking to me like I'm a pop star, 'cos it makes me feel like I'm becoming two dimensional.' He also told writer Clare Kleinedler how he had great trepidation about his increasing star persona: 'That whole idea of being Thom Yorke, "the personality" . . . I don't want to die having been just that. That whole thing that most pop stars are desperately trying to attain immortality through their cult of personality . . . this phenomenon, this Sunday review section, glossy front page . . . It's like "No!, actually. No!" I don't want to be remembered for this, I want to be remembered for doing pieces of work that people liked, and other than that I don't really want to know. I'm not into this for immortality's sake. Sixty years from now, I'm going to be dead, and that will be that.' Jonny was rather more satisfied – he had fulfilled his ambition to say 'wanker' and 'bollocks' on every major radio station they appeared on.

As well as the dates with REM, Radiohead played scores of other gigs across the world in support of *The Bends*. Shortly after the REM tour, on 4 October, while they were preparing for their first gig in support of the mid-Western folk-punk of Soul Asylum at the Ogden Theater in Denver, all their gear was stolen from their van. Although the insurance replaced their instruments 'with nice new things', it created a major inconvenience. That night, Thom and Jonny performed a rare acoustic set, while the other three took the night off. Typically contrary, Thom actually liked the experience of theft: 'I quite enjoyed that,' he told *Select*, 'because everyone felt sorry for us all day. We went to this restaurant and got the best tables, free pizzas. I was walking down the street and this tramp says "Sorry to hear about your gear."' Jonny was not so charitable, saying, 'I hope their next shit is a porcupine.'

Dates in Japan were fantastically attended. As with many western bands, Radiohead were welcomed in the hotel lobby every morning by dozens of fans who gave them presents and chatted shyly. Occasionally they would go out to eat with the nicer ones. 'They're not pushy,' Jonny told *Raygun*, 'they'll take photographs of me and Japanese girls, pictures of myself with a stranger times a hundred.' One amazing story Thom heard was that a small clique of Japanese girl fans were following Radiohead around the globe every tour, and allegedly paying for their travelling expenses by prostitution.

The nicest of these fans were actually Epic Records employees, who felt that Phil didn't get enough limelight (Jonny is usually the favourite, especially with younger girls) so they formed 'The Phil Selway Fan Club' and held a dinner in

his honour (on arriving one girl said 'I find your beady eyes intolerably attractive'). The band dined with the thirteen fan club members, eating Phil's favourite meal of steak and potatoes, before playing some party games, the winner of which got to give Phil a hug. The club was initially inspired by some Radiohead fans mistaking Phil for the band's bus driver and asking him if he could get the group's autographs. Another tale from America relates how Phil was wearing a Radiohead T-shirt, and a shop cashier said 'Hey, Radiohead are amazing! I think they are playing around here tonight . . . are you going?' The Japanese fan club was later disbanded, in typical Radiohead fashion, because the founders worried too much about upsetting the other band members.

'I think I'd make a very good member of the Royal family, shaking hands with individuals in large crowds – "Oh hello, I play bass, get pissed and talk about myself."'

Jonny found the constant press obligations tiresome: 'I got really despairing in Canada because I hadn't seen an instrument in weeks but had still been talking about Radiohead every day. I started ranting about how we should perhaps sign to an obscure indie label and just play loads of concerts in England and do more recording.' Colin seemed far more affable and able to take the whole spectacle in his stride: 'I like getting drunk and meeting people and eating good food and finding out about different cultures and what people do. I think I'd make a very good member of the Royal family, shaking hands with individuals in large crowds – "Oh hello, I play bass, get pissed and talk about myself."'

Thom was not so patient. In Vancouver they were playing a promotional gig to a largely uninterested audience made up of record industry types. One table near the front were not listening and were getting progressively louder and more anti-social as the night wore on. Finally, Thom had had enough and shouted, 'Look, we've gone all round the world on this tour, but you are the rudest fuckers we've ever met.' There was complete silence for a few seconds, before the rest of the crowd started throwing punches at the rowdy table. The entire evening ended in a massive bar room brawl, whilst a bemused Radiohead vainly tried to play 'Fake Plastic Trees' in the background.

Of course, Radiohead being Radiohead, things did not always go to plan. The band, and Thom in particular, suffered a variety of physical ailments on tour, where the poor diet and constant travelling often proved debilitating to the lead singer's fragile constitution. After suffering problems with fluid in his ears, he was worried about going deaf, and he seemed to be first in line if any bug or illness was going around. As Phil explained, with the extra demands on Thom, he was often the one who felt the most drained: 'When you're out on tour, it's a prime time to become a hypochondriac. It's the very nature of it – you get very worn out. Especially for somebody like Thom, everyone looks to Thom for the voice, they're really impressed by the voice. So, there are so many things that can affect that. He gets slightly run down and his voice won't produce what it should. I think, it's almost paralysing in a way.'

'I wouldn't say that we are a collection of invalids or anything... We are no sicker and probably much healthier than a lot of other groups.'

Jonny was by now suffering from repetitive strain injury on his right arm, from the demanding way he played guitar – he often left the stage with bloody cuts from the lashing he had given his six strings. Some observers read his addition of an arm brace as some kind of fey fashion accessory (like Morrissey's infamous ear piece) but he genuinely needed it. At the same time, at one show he had a row of red lights flashing down it! He also began to wear a huge pair of 1970s headphones, on doctor's orders, after his ears bled for two weeks during some American dates. With regard to the brace he once said, 'It's conceited to deny there's any affectation . . . I enjoy putting the arm brace on before I play. It's like taping up your fingers before a boxing match. It's a ritual.' Jonny has also been known to bring a tamagotchi on stage. There were rumours that he played his guitar with a vibrator, but these were unfounded – it was actually a finger-massager.

To help avoid the kind of personality clashes that had caused problems on earlier tours, such as the near implosion in Mexico, the band travelled almost entirely separately. Colin regularly travelled with the road crew, while Thom and Jonny would go to gigs with their manager. Before and after the show, the band were rarely in the same place at the same time. Despite Thom's sickly reputation, Colin denied in *Circus* that Radiohead were any more road weaklings than any other band: 'I don't think that we are that unhealthy, to be honest with you. It's more like when you start off you don't know how much your body will or will not tolerate. So you try everything as far as doing shows and your body draws a line in the sand . . . I wouldn't say that we are a collection of invalids or anything . . . We are no sicker and probably much healthier than a lot of other groups.'

'Rehab's not a luxury we can afford.' **Thom**

One aspect of their touring and general lifestyle that Radiohead quickly became well known for is their utter lack of rock 'n' roll excess. The press have often mocked them for their mundanity, but in their defence, it makes a refreshing change in an industry characterised by excess. Often referred to as 'the most polite band in musicdom', they have repeatedly avoided the bacchanalian extremes that are often assumed to be compulsory. After all, this was the band who had delayed world domination to go to college. They were all highly educated, and this was reflected in their tour bus antics, or rather lack of them. Jonny was often immersed deep in his aforementioned audio tapes of the classics. They all read books for relaxation off stage – Colin once took a voluminous book called *A Historical Study : The Collapse Of British Power* on tour because 'I'm working on my knowledge of history.' His brother was sent *The Sayings Of The Vikings* from EMI Norway to celebrate *The Bends* going gold – he read it voraciously.

Many early Radiohead interviews dwelt on their passion for contract bridge, with talk of special pocket bridge tables and tips on the game itself. Jonny is apparently an accomplished kite flyer. He is also an obsessive crossword fanatic, having been preoccupied with them ever since completing an unfinished one just before his father's death. 'It's just mental masturbation, I guess', so much so that he has to get English crosswords faxed over whilst on tour in America because he finds the Stateside versions too insulting. They regularly come back from tour with bags filled with unopened alcohol from their hospitality rider, although they admit that heavy drinking has become a more regular feature since the mid-nineties. Backstage they usually have a settee in their dressing room. They have three simple rules when on tour: '(1) Be Nice. (2) Take it outside. (3) Walk away.' They decide the set list by playing a game of 'sounds like . . . ' (eg: 'sounds like 'Groove' – Prove . . . Yourself). On one tour in America, their support band trashed the dressing room, and Radiohead tidied it up. Their drummer is a former Samaritan. Their bass player is called Colin.

'I threw stuff around and threw my amp around and drum kit and ended up with blood all over my face and things. I cried for about two hours afterwards.'

The nearest they seem to have come to a genuine rock 'n' roll blow out was when Thom once walked offstage in Munich, after smashing some gear up in a rage. Unfortunately, things were not as decadent as they appeared – he had felt ill but was forced into performing: 'The doctor came round at four o'clock because every time you don't do a show, you have to get a doctor's certificate saying you are too sick to do a show, just like school, so you have a fucking sicknote. If you don't get the sicknote, you get sued for thousands and thousands and thousands of pounds . . . of course the doctor was paid for by the promoter. He says, "you're fine, you're fine to do the show," and I was like, "I can't fucking speak, let alone sing."' That day it had been snowing and despite the three foot drifts, people had still driven for hours to get to the show. So Thom was determined to have a go at performing, but three songs in, he collapsed. The *NME* blazed the headline 'Thom's Temper Tantrum' and grossly offended the singer with a fictional story of how he had stormed off and sulked backstage, refusing to go back on. He later explained 'I just got really fucking freaked out. I got tunnel vision and I don't really know what happened. I threw stuff around and threw my amp around and drum kit and ended up with blood all over my face and things. I cried for about two hours afterwards. I want people to know what happened that night. I'm sure no one gives a fuck and I'm sure the *NME* don't give a fuck, but what they wrote in that piece hurt me more than anything else anyone has ever written about me.'

'This is probably very un-rock 'n' roll to say but our biggest concern is the amount of flying that we do. Jet lag and the poor circulation in the cabins of these planes is hard on the larynx.'

Whilst other bands suffered from various excesses with what is euphemistically called 'nervous exhaustion' in the trade, Radiohead have slightly more mundane worries: 'This is probably very un-rock 'n' roll to say but our biggest concern is the amount of flying that we do. Jet lag and the poor circulation in the cabins of these planes is hard on the larynx.'

It is not that they haven't tried the rock star lifestyle, in moderation, but it was not for them. Jonny admitted to trying drugs on one occasion, but needed his manager to come in and 'talk him down' because he wasn't enjoying it: 'I felt this insanity growing in my head. If you feel that bad the morning after, why bother with it?' Instead, they have chosen to worry about things like cookware – Ed: 'My mum bought me a fish steamer for Christmas, and that was the most exciting thing ever.'

They have publicly admonished the moshers at their shows, and frown upon any extreme behaviour at their gigs – some shows have signs saying 'Radiohead request no crowd-surfing'. On a tour of South America, they stopped in a town where a huge decadent festival was taking place – with typical Radiohead panache, they took a wrong turn and walked for hours along the only street that led away from the party. They ended up spending the night in a small English-style pub over a few quiet pints. They eat cereal and juice for breakfast when most bands are still out partying – and there is always a jar of Marmite on the catering table. They used to carry video cameras on tour to capture their experiences, then they bought computers and spent hours sitting in front of them at home. Instead of flying to each gig, the neurotic Thom and Jonny travel by coach so that they can catch up on their reading.

Unlike certain other groups, not even a sibling relationship provides any source of tension. Colin and his younger brother Jonny, whom he always calls Jonathan, have never publicly had a row on tour. 'I think there are a couple of people at EMI who wouldn't mind us going on a 'stress mis-management' course,' Colin once said to *Hot Press*, 'because inter-band violence seems to be all the rage at the moment. It's a standard question we get asked and I always feel a bit guilty saying, "Well, no actually, we haven't hospitalised each other recently." The trouble is that beyond the normal brotherly thing, I respect him as a person and a musician.' The worst friction recorded between the two brothers dates to way back when they were at primary school, when Colin would change the paints around in their pots, ensuring that a colour-blind Jonny would create some disturbing pictures as a result. Colin claims the most scary thing Jonny has ever done on tour is talk in his sleep. Band violence is unheard of, and despite their moments of tension, there have been no personnel changes in over the twelve years of their existence, they have kept the same management and Thom has been with the same girl.

'I think there are a couple of people at EMI who wouldn't mind us going on a 'stress mis-management' course.'

All their hard-earned royalties are quickly placed into a high-interest deposit account ('So if we're dropped, we'll have enough money to put out another album on our own label'), and after Thom's bank account swelled from the funds from *Pablo Honey*, all he bought was a Sony Walkman. Colin bought some bass lessons. Their record company were so frustrated by the band's total lack of extravagance that they offered them a clothing budget. Ed bought one white shirt. Thom (who claims he 'could shop for England') went and spent about £30 in an Oxfam shop.

Groupies are a complete no-no as well. After one gig in Dallas, Ed was cornered by a curvaceous female fan who was salivating over her potential rock star catch. She told him her parents were away for a week, that she lived just around the corner from the venue, and that she had a big bag of coke with her. The band even had a day off the next morning. Ed said no. Another time, a naked girl knocked on Jonny's hotel room door in Los Angeles, about which the guitarist reported, 'Luckily, I wasn't in.' Phil admits to having withdrawal symptoms when he's on tour and doesn't see his wife for weeks. Jonny is similarly uninterested: 'I've never taken advantage of the opportunity of one-night stands. It's like treating sex like sneezing. Sex is a fairly disgusting sort of tufted, smelly-area kind of activity, which is too intimate to engage in with strangers. I'm all for erotic in terms of imagination, but the physical side is something different.'

In fact, Thom intensely dislikes the whole groupie scene: 'Being surrounded by all these fucking harpies, witches, warlocks, and fucking weirdos everywhere you walk, who are saying whatever they think is the appropriate thing to say to you. You are going to fucking lose it. You either can go elsewhere and choose your friends, or you're doomed.' He once said he 'had never met a beautiful woman he liked' and that he would do anything to avoid contact with them (a comment he later called 'rude and silly'). He has also said, 'I tend to run away if it's anything beyond them saying they like the music. We were at a single sex school, so . . . you know . . . Anyway I have someone that I love, so it's . . . nice.' With some justification, Radiohead have been called the anti-Chippendales.

'I'm all for erotic in terms of imagination, but the physical side is something different.'

On the other hand, the group are painstakingly considerate towards their fans. Thom carries a satchel of fan letters around the world with him, and replies whenever he can. When the band found out a mother and daughter had driven several hundred miles in the vain hope of obtaining a ticket to a sold-out show, they took them backstage and gave them the VIP treatment all night. They always try to make some time to talk to people at shows: 'When I was sixteen,' Ed said in *The Diamondback*, 'the bands that I was into, I would hope that they would be cool and would treat me nice, because I'm a fan of what they're doing. It's really taking what you were like at fifteen or sixteen or whatever and making into "Do as you would be done by."'

There are very few interviews where Radiohead are openly being offensive or difficult on record, other than the early batch of articles where Thom openly criticised his contemporaries in the music press. The Greenwoods, known as the 'Greenwood sisters' for their complete lack of any macho qualities are particularly polite. The most unco-operative Jonny ever got was when he told one writer, '*Pablo Honey* was our first time in the studio, so what can you expect?

The Beatles' first album was almost all covers.' About the most rock 'n' roll thing Radiohead have ever done is to get their friends to pretend to be them in phone interviews. Indeed, for any extremes you have to look to their fans, like the one who asked Colin to sign her arm and then turned up at the next gig with the signature tattooed over the biro original. Indeed, the most excessive the band seem to get is when they actually come *off* tour, when they admit the notorious 'tour decompression' makes them hard to live with.

In the light of this absence of excess, plus the band's university educations and their comfortable middle class backgrounds, much has been made of Radiohead being a safe, middle-class band. Like Blur before them (who incidentally were comprehensive school educated, but fell foul of the media's view of them as coming from the middle-class intelligentsia in contrast to Oasis's brutal working class world), Radiohead have been subject to derisory comment, particularly in the light of Thom's often highly troubled lyrics. Clichéd and tired as it is, they are often criticised by the school of thought that claims you cannot write true angst unless you are a poor, tortured bedsit poet. Thom found very early on that critics were highly unforgiving about his apparent 'qualifications'. Rightly so, he ridiculed this ludicrous line of attack: 'The middle-class thing has never been relevant. We live in Oxford, and in Oxford we're fucking lower class. It's all relative . . . The thing that winds me up about the middle-class question is the presumption that a middle-class upbringing is a balanced environment, when in fact, domestic situations are not relevant to class. A bad domestic situation is a bad domestic situation. It's just such a fucking warped perspective on things.'

However, to be fair to their critics, Radiohead have not always helped themselves. While most bands are content to hail the merits of tour mayhem, booze, birds and bonks, Radiohead are rather more refined in interview. They regularly started sentences with phrases like 'As Arthur Miller said in his autobiography,' or 'I think a good place to start would be Noam Chomsky.' Poetry is regularly quoted, and Jonny has expressed his love of the poems of Philip Larkin, naming the song 'Lozenge Of Love' after a line from his poem 'Sad Steps'. He even once read out Larkin's 'Home Is So Sad' on BBC Radio One. Thom has shrunk his middle initial to a small case 'e' in honour of e.e. cummings. It seems that Radiohead are just not a normal type of band, as Colin once explained: 'We are not really a party group. We don't do any drugs or drink heavily at all. We don't really even stay out late.'

< chapter: 7 >

YOU'RE TURNING INTO SOMETHING YOU'RE NOT

'It's a sickness, because people look at you weird and talk to you weird.'
Thom

'People sometimes ask me if I'm happy and I tell them to fuck off. If I was happy, I'd be in a fucking car advert. A lot of people think they're happy, and then they live these boring lives and do the same things every day. But one day they wake up and realise that they haven't lived yet. I'd much rather celebrate the highs and lows of everyday life than try to deny them.' **Thom**

As the band's popularity has grown a cult has developed around Thom Yorke that makes various flawed claims. Certain sections of the media have marked Thom as another in a long line of pop miserabilists, nervous, angst-ridden, petrified of fame. One writer said he looked like 'a nervous breakdown gone solo'. The extreme line in this approach listed him as the most likely musician to commit suicide, the next rock martyr. He is supposedly the new anti-hero for a generation, the genius on the outside, the tortured artist for the millennium. These theories are based on a number of observations.

First, starting your career with an autobiographical song called 'Creep' and deprecating yourself as a weirdo and a loser is not a good way of gaining a reputation for sanity. (After this hit, Thom received a letter from a prisoner on Death Row, saying how much he identified with Thom, and how he understood all his feelings; he even said that the voices in his head had agreed with Thom. Receiving a letter from a convicted killer deeply disturbed him for months afterwards – 'I felt like someone had walked over my grave.') Observers have looked to the repeated malaise in Thom's lyrics, the abyss of emotional trauma he often stares down in his songs. Despite repeated denials that not all of his songs were despairing, Thom did little to help his defence by writing *The Bends*, one of the decade's most morose and sad albums. Even he could not deny its tortured isolation and bleak vulnerability. Some called it 'the depressivess soundtrack to the nineties'.

Secondly, observers have pointed to current climate and the media-christened 'culture of despair'. The end of the millennium psychosis, the death of Kurt Cobain, the prevalence of heroin in the West Coast music scene, the disappearance of Richey Manic. Nirvana's desperate *In Utero* and the Manic Street Preachers' harrowing *The Holy Bible* albums have been cited as pivotal records in this climate of thought, indications that fundamental misery underpinned pop music. *The Bends*, despite being less first person, less diary-based and vaguer than these two albums, now made up a supposed trio of morbidity and angst for a shattered generation. People expressed concern about how a man as fragile as Thom could write such a litany of anxiety and yet still survive. The renaissance of nihilism, first popularised by nineteenth-century Russian philosophers, perhaps reflected this general cultural malaise – nihilism was chic. Even the *Six O Clock News* on the BBC featured pieces on the subject, while the tabloids had a field day every time another rock star overdosed or died. Thom, it was claimed, fitted perfectly into the picture.

Thirdly, observers have identified Thom's apparent inability to cope with the trappings of celebrity. He hates the public restrictions imposed by the fame that his profile has brought. He despises groupie sex, he struggles to contain his contempt for an industry in which he is inextricably involved. He particularly hates award ceremonies, which epitomise for him the shallowness of the industry; he once voiced his feelings to *Studio Brussels Radio*: 'There's two ways to be a popstar. One way is, you go to the film openings, the fashion shows, you are seen to be a popstar . . . but I've got a problem with that, 'cos I don't, I'm not interested in these people. The reason why I am not interested in these people is 'cos they spend the whole fucking time going to these fucking openings to be seen, to be pop stars or whatever it is . . . How does it feel to be a popstar?

'You do sometimes get the feeling that you're just one more element in the entertainment industry's desperate attempt to distract people from the fact that their lives are [messed] up.'

It's a useful thing to have, 'cos it's a way of part of what I do, but . . . it's pretty . . . a fucking lame thing to put on your passport.' When questioned about the hordes of celebrities that often attended his band's gigs, he was utterly dismissive: 'I hope there is a difference between people in a sweaty club listening to a band playing and the hype of award ceremonies. Self-congratulation is ugly. I don't have a problem with whoever coming to our shows. Are they fashionable? Are we? I don't think we'll ever pass the film-premiere test – we wouldn't look good in *US* magazine. America has a very fucked view of fame anyway. It's mind-bending but irrelevant. I'd much rather watch the news or go out and get drunk or try and sort my home out.' He has also said 'You do sometimes get the feeling that you're just one more element in the entertainment industry's desperate attempt to distract people from the fact that their lives are [messed] up.' He once admitted that waking up to see a gold record in his lounge meant that he 'kinda felt like a rock star then . . . briefly'.

Fourthly, people have highlighted Thom's own admissions about how much he worries, how he likes to destabilise his surroundings if they are too secure, and his repeated public expressions of his fears and doubts – 'The creative process can only work in a state of panic.' Also, Radiohead are famously self-critical, Thom more so than anyone. When *The Bends* won so many plaudits at the end of the year polls in 1995 , Thom was pleased but simply said ' It wasn't that good.' The band members used to joke that whenever Radiohead were criticised they weren't surprised because they had usually already aired the particular reservation a thousand times themselves. In interviews, Thom has often seemed filled with self-loathing, depressed and weary. Even the more mundane things of life seem to trouble him, if his interviews are to be believed: '[I was] trying to sit still . . . over Christmas. Sit in front of the television for more than 20 minutes without just shouting at it and getting up and moving out again. And I find it very, very, very, very difficult indeed. Other than that, I play with my Macintosh. All day long. Very sad.'

He had clearly done an enormous amount of self-analysis himself, and this did not always come out overly-optimistic: 'There's a pervading sense of loneliness I've had since the day I was born. Maybe a lot of other people feel the same way, but I'm not about to run up and down the street asking everybody if they're as lonely as I am. I'd probably get locked up.' He has also said, 'I'm obsessed with the idea that I'm completely losing touch with who I am, and I've come to the conclusion that there isn't anything to Thom Yorke other than the guy that makes those painful songs.'

Finally, his physical appearance, with his lazy eye, his diminutive stature, and his sickly pallor and susceptibility to illness on the road meant that all of the above alleged mental problems were exacerbated by a supposed physical fragility. His fingernails, always bitten to the quick, reinforced this reputation for nervousness. How could this man, who looked like the 'before' picture in a bodybuilding advert, cope with such stresses? Standing waif-like, next to the 6 foot 5 inch Ed, Thom, with his pallid face, often seemed too feeble to cope, while on stage his ravaged movements and crunched face only seemed to confirm this impression. One particularly appalling incident occurred when he appeared on the front cover of the London listings magazine, *Time Out*, and a reader wrote in complaining that photographs of 'people who look like that' should not be used in the media.

One particular article in the *Melody Maker* pushed this melodramatic view of Thom Yorke, the rock martyr to the limit. The piece described him as no more than a borderline misogynist, self-hating and on the brink. It looked at other potential rock martyrs, Eddie Vedder ('too robust'), Courtney Love ('plainly indestructible'), and concluded that Thom had to be next to put himself on slab at the morgue. With stunningly bad taste, the piece stated, 'There is clearly only one serious contender. Spindly, spiteful, wracked with self loathing – and soon to be so before the eyes of millions. Another fiercely burning star, destined to go nova and implode. Another black hole into which to tip our most grievous emotions and see them dazzle . . . Thom, 26, looks the part. He's short delicate fey, but unlike Kurt and Ritchie . . . he is vulnerable, twisted and convulses on stage . . . Thom looks like a fine prospect, another martyr in the making, another young blade ready to slash himself to pieces. Too fast to live, too young to die, eh?'

Apart from being highly offensive, theories like this are rather tiresome. They also perpetuate myths rather than trying to reveal the full person. When asked directly if Thom is really like that away from the public eye, Colin told

Radiohead on the streets of New York.

Hot Press, 'If you caught him while he was writing his lyrics, [yes,] but otherwise he's a reasonably upbeat sort of person.' The rest of the band have also said that in private he has a very puerile sense of humour, and can be childishly foolish. Thom himself has often denied this analysis of himself. He was particularly upset about the piece in *Melody Maker*. After this he stopped reading his own press, and refused for some time to interview for that magazine.

'Oh, for Christ sake, I did not write this album for people to slash their fucking wrists to.'

This reading of *The Bends* particularly riled him: 'Oh, for Christ sake, I did not write this album for people to slash their fucking wrists to.' He also said, '*The Bends* isn't my confessional. And I don't want it used as an aid to stupidity and fuck-wittery . . . It's not an excuse to wallo. I don't want to know about your depression – if you write to me, I will write back, angrily, telling you not to give into all that shit.' 'Shut up, fuck off and go and buy the Smith's back catalogue instead. Our music is of no use to you.' The irony is that in these outspoken defences, he is both fuelling the difficult pop star image, and adding to the sense of isolation felt by the many outsiders that admire him.

It frustrates him that the humour in his songs is not often seen. 'The song 'The Bends' is completely jokey, I'm completely taking the piss. None of that stuff had even happened to us when we wrote it.' However, as his lyrics are at times hard to decipher and filled with bizarre, dark imagery, observers can be forgiven for jumping to conclusions. Thom claims that even apparently morbid music can be uplifting.

Many observers have noticed that with Radiohead's growing success, Thom has actually become more settled, and less harassed. As the wheels of the Radiohead machine grind ever faster and bigger, its success has released him, rather than ensnared him. The tour with REM undoubtedly helped, but his own innate sense of reality is the grounding foundation, as it is with the rest of the band as well. 'I'm in this business, I choose to be in this business, but I also choose to be in this business on my terms, you know.' As for any thoughts of suicide, Thom is totally dismissive: 'I love life, I really do.'

He even once said the only worry he gets is when he will 'get into a panic . . . get really nervous [thinking] that I'm not weird enough, and then I think, "Hang on. This is completely ridiculous. What's the point of that?" There are groups that expend so much time and energy proving how larger-than-life they are . . . for who? For whose benefit? If you're going to do it, prove it in your music and shut up.'

Ultimately, Thom Yorke is no new messiah, no suicidal tortured artist sitting in his bedsit, surrounded by scrawled notes with a million pounds of unspent, unwanted royalties under his pillow. He acknowledges the inherent difficulties of what he does, and in so doing ensures that he will always be in control: 'What frightens me is the idea that what Radiohead do is basically packaged back to people in the form of entertainment, to play in their car stereos on their way to work . . . but then I should shut the fuck up because it's pop music and it's not anything more than that.'

• • •

With the international dates, the growing cult surrounding Thom Yorke, and the longevity of sales for *The Bends*, the end of 1995 saw Radiohead in their strongest position ever. The success was bolstered enormously by the string of singles they released in 1995 to support the album. The Top 30 success of 'High And Dry' was followed by the May release of 'Fake Plastic Trees'.

Unexpectedly, an acoustic version of this track can be heard in the background of the film *Clueless*, whereupon one of the characters in the movie calls the song 'cry baby music'. Surprisingly, Thom was flattered, saying, 'The characters in that film aren't the kind of people I'd want to like Radiohead. They're just average, two-dimensional Beverly Hills kids, and the person who is actually listening to us in the film is the only three-dimensional character. So the answer is: "Fuck you, we're for 3D people!"' Colin, ever the intellectual, and with his tongue pushed firmly into his cheek, said, 'There's is an early modern English literature analogy to that, which is the poetry of complaint. Basically it was an oral tradition in which the peasants bemoaned their losses. And of course complaint can also mean illness. So, it's good to see Alicia has a good grounding in literature.' The single also held fond memories for him: 'There was a time when we did the Conan O' Brien talk show for the second time. We played "Fake Plastic Trees", then we went for a meal, got hammered and went back to the hotel. I was in bed, turned on the TV and there we were. It was just really,

really good; all the quiet bits were really quiet and all the loud bits were really loud. That's our first three and a half minutes of TV that I was really proud of.' The single reached number 20 in the UK.

Next up was 'Just', released in early September, which some critics claimed was a little too similar to Magazine's 'Shot By Both Sides', but this did not stop the track reaching number 19 in the charts. Then came 'Lucky', Radiohead's contribution to the *Help!* album, a fund-raiser for victims of the conflict in former Yugoslavia. For this project, a collection of British music top names came together to record an entire album in less than a week, with the finished album being available in the shops the following weekend. While most publicity went to the contributions of people like Oasis, Paul Weller and Paul McCartney, there were several respectful nods to Radiohead's contribution, 'Lucky'. The band themselves were delighted with the track – they particularly enjoyed the creative process behind this song, crammed into an intensive and once-only five-hour deadline. 'Some songs are completely automatic,' Thom told *Addicted To Noise*, 'like "Lucky", where there was absolutely no thought process or anything involved. We just played it one day and that was it. I played the chords once around and everyone joined in and that was the song . It was just frightening, frankly.' Thom later admitted that Jonny's guitar work on that track reduced him to 'a gibbering wreck'. In response to this single, *Melody Maker* wrote, 'Radiohead are no longer capable of anything other than brilliance.' The matching video promo depicted casualties of the Bosnian war and reduced Thom to tears when he first saw it. Amazingly, despite the charity focus of the single, Radio One refused to play it, calling it 'too abrasive'. Thom in particular was gutted. The song stalled at number 51.

For an album that had been criticised for not having any singles on it during its inception, *The Bends* threw up an astonishing array of stunning records. Last out was the closing 'Street Spirit (Fade Out)'. Winding up the project with such a languid and yet formidable track only served to reinforce the popular and critical opinion of Radiohead – that they were now as versatile and accomplished as any current rock band in the world. Strangely, Thom has said that he was inspired to write the song when he got off a bus and saw some dead baby sparrows on the pavement, next to their eggshells. Again Radio One barely supported the release, but it still charted at number 5. With this single came the fruits of a sudden rush of creativity that occurred – two brilliant B-sides, 'Bishop's Robes' and 'Talk Show Host' which was the band's first venture into trip hop. It was hard to imagine this was the same band who had released 'Creep'.

• • •

'I can't really see the difference between shooting a video and making a car advert.' **Thom**

A contributary reason for the new esteem for Radiohead, apart simply from the quality of 'Street Spirit', was the beautiful accompanying video. Filmed with a military high-speed camera running at thousands of frames a second, its mixture of real time and slow motion footage, coated in beautiful black and white tones and featuring dancers, dogs and steel caravans, was simply stunning. Radiohead had already earned quite a reputation for their video work. Despite abhorring the obscene amounts of money required (many promos cost far more than an entire album), they seem to acknowledge their necessity. They often choose directors with no previous experience of film work, they always opt for unusual and demanding treatments, and the overall effect is often breath-taking. 'Fake Plastic Trees' was like some bizarre supermarket of cosmetic surgery, 'Just' contained a scene that became famous where the man lying on a street reveals something so horrible and so devastating that the by-standers are floored, yet the viewer cannot hear what it is as the promo's sub-titles stop before he speaks (the band have *never* revealed what he said, despite constant requests). Radiohead videos are always compelling, but often do not make perfect sense, and, certainly during *The Bends* project, they substantially complement their recorded output. One time MTV Vice President of Music, Lewis Largent, said in the media that, 'All their videos are intriguing. Everybody has a different interpretation of them. The videos aren't cut and dried . . . that sort of mystery makes them watchable time and time again. You can watch [some of them] a hundred times and not figure it all out.'

The band's artwork similarly has depth. Much of it is created by Thom's college friend Dan Rickwood, with Thom's assistance. 'Fake Plastic Trees' shows a woman from a Brazilian soap opera with her eyes blacked out, because Thom liked the idea of mixing fame with anonymity. 'Just' was video stills of the backstreets of Plymouth, with lettering taken from number plates, fire hydrants, street signs and other scraps, which roughly joined together spelt Radiohead. *The Bends* album cover is chock-full of peculiar images – the inflated belly of a Gulf War soldier, people walking along a road in New Zealand, a face scribbled by Thom, Japanese car salesmen, Japanese weather symbols, and an old television logo. Throughout their career, Radiohead have continued to produce fascinating artwork – symbols, bizarre images and obscure phrases litter their

'What's the fucking point in painting or drawing this thing in this way when I can go and buy a camera for two quid and do it like that?'

sleeves and liners. Thom's own scrawlings are regular features of the sleeves, but he has side-stepped any compliments by saying 'I can't draw. They told me I couldn't draw at art college – at least I'm honest about it. My whole argument at art college was, "What's the fucking point in painting or drawing this thing in this way when I can go and buy a camera for two quid and do it like that? Why should I bother drawing it?" I could never quite work out how I blagged my way into art college anyway.'

• • •

When 'Street Spirit (Fade Out)' charted, and although it was to sixteen places out of the Top Twenty in only its second week, *The Bends* jumped up fifteen places to its highest position yet thus far at number 4 in the album listings. It had already been released for over ten months. This was the start of a remarkable growth in commercial success and critical applause that transformed Radiohead from a band that was highly revered into one that was being talked of as a historically classic group. While the rest of Britain had been captivated by the Britpop phenomenon and the Oasis–Blur rivalry, which peaked with the simultaneous release of singles from each band in August 1995, Radiohead had been touring hard. Initially the plaudits of the Britpop era went elsewhere, but Radiohead were happy not to be lumped in with this crowd, and by the start of 1996, the spotlight was turning onto them. By now, of course, *The Bends* had scored five Top 30 British hits and sold over a million copies worldwide.

Part of the reason for *The Bends'* resurgence during the end of year period was the run of accolades it received in music magazines' end of year polls, with many of them calling it the album of 1995. This had aroused curiosity in a public eager for new sounds, and the release of 'Street Spirit' had touched this nerve, helped by some bullish and astute marketing from their record label, which included Radiohead's first TV advertising campaign and press saturation.

Thom in Dublin.

The band's credentials were further enhanced in February 1996 when they were nominated for three Brit Awards – best British group, best British album and best promo for 'Just' – but, surprisingly, they won nothing. This did nothing for Thom's hatred or awards ceremonies. He told *Raygun*: 'A complete and utter disgusting charade. Yes of course it pissed me off that Oasis got loads of awards and we got none. But it was worse than that 'cos I realised for the first time what kind of business the music industry is. I was sitting there in a world of ugly men in suits, who were accompanied by women that weren't their wives and who were wearing cocktail dresses that didn't fit properly. All bands were so far gone that they didn't have a clue as to what they were saying. Very humiliating.' Rather more humorously, the band were invited to play the *Smash Hits* Poll Winners Party, where viewers watched the bizarre sight of Take That, Boyzone and East 17 playing alongside a glum Radiohead blasting out 'My Iron Lung'.

Nevertheless, *The Bends* appeared to have massive appeal to a huge diversity of music lovers. Die-hard Radiohead fans were now joined by much older listeners, REM fans, and the casual buyer who had caught them on MTV or at the Brits. The album was even popular with ravers, who apparently liked to play the record as their post-pill come-down soundtrack. The band were delighted with the full and final recognition that was now coming their way: 'We're incredibly proud that the record is doing so well,' Colin said in the press. 'We've only had one *NME* cover, which is ridiculous for a band who've sold three million records, but it proves that people are buying the album because they've heard through word-of-mouth that it's good.' Ed was taken aback by the change: 'I was away for four weeks, away from Britain, and when I got back, there's this totally different vibe about us. We were really being talked about.' As a consequence, Ed says that '*The Bends* completely and utterly changed my life.'

Colin told the press an even more comical tale of *The Bends'* peculiarly diverse appeal: 'The weirdest people in the weirdest places are united by that record. The Daisies, who share the same management as us, got stopped in their van in London on the day of an IRA bomb. They were surrounded by armed police who wanted to know who the hell they were. Then they mentioned our name and this copper with a gun goes, "Oh, *The Bends* is brilliant," and the mood relaxed instantly.'

• • •

Before starting work on a third album, Radiohead played yet more dates in the first half of 1996 in support of *The Bends*. Before that, Phil spent some time with his wife, Thom travelled around Europe, Ed holidayed in India, Jonny buried his head in yet more books and Colin moved to London. In February, Thom and Brian Eno collected the Freddie Mercury Award for the *Help!* album at the Brits, and in the same month the band announced they would be supporting the Rock The Vote campaign. They were also to contribute a Nellee Hooper remix of 'Talk Show Host' and 'Exit Music For A Film' to the forthcoming soundtrack for the film *William Shakespeare's Romeo & Juliet*, starring the latest teen heart-throb, Leonardo Di Caprio. Then, more overseas dates were played, including some in Europe with the Bluetones and a headline slot at Bristol Sound City.

'I mean, we're headlining T in the Park, and they were saying, "Do you want to go on after the Sex Pistols or after Lou Reed?" It was all very unreal.'

By now their live show was fearsomely tight and powerful: *Melody Maker* said 'Radiohead are staggering . . . tonight they're blazing, so compacted and honed to impact by the smallness of this venue . . . "Plant Telex" is pretty much state of the art nineties rock, certainly throwing a horribly revealing light on the rest of this week's paltry, crippled indie fare.' A headline show at Glasgow's huge T in the Park festival also followed, for which they warmed up for with a coupe of secret shows in their hometown of Oxford. As an indication that their success had hardly gone to their heads, Jonny told one journalist how he still found it strange: 'I mean, we're headlining T in the Park, and they were saying, "Do you want to go on after the Sex Pistols or after Lou Reed?" It was all very unreal.'

Then it was off for their tenth stint in America, this time supporting the queen of mainstream 'grunge', Alanis Morissette. Despite the seemingly inappropriate clash of styles, Jonny loved it: 'That was fun, that was so surreal and peculiar that we just felt very detached from everything that was happening. This tour came up, playing in front of 13-year-old girls, and we thought "Let's go and do a Pink Floyd in front of them."' Once these dates were completed, Radiohead finally retreated back to Oxfordshire, to contemplate work on their next record.

< c h a p t e r : 8 >

WE HOPE YOUR RULES AND WISDOM CHOKE YOU

'Take as long as you want, record it wherever you want, with whoever you want.' **Parlophone**

'Our creative process is driven by disappointment with past work we've done.' **Jonny**

As with *The Bends*, the recording sessions for Radiohead's third album were prolonged, stressful but ultimately highly creative. Again, early rehearsals and demos were completed at the band's converted fruit shed in Oxfordshire, during January 1996. This time, the band had opted for producing themselves, with the able assistance of Nigel Godrich, who had been engineer on their previous album. He was the same age as the band and had similar musical tastes, so he was asked to guide them through the hurdles of the forthcoming sessions. The self-production option was not because they had no alternative. REM's producer Scott Litt had offered his skills, but had hastily withdrawn them soon after, telling the band that they didn't need him. Other high-profile producers had said the same. The first thing Nigel Godrich was told to do was 'draw a wish list' of his ideal recording equipment, and was then given $140,000 to go and buy it. He actually under-spent by some way, but nevertheless managed to fill the fruit shed, christened Canned Applause by the band, with state-of-the-art gear. The band relished this environment:

'Most times, you go into a recording studio, and you can still smell the body odour from Whitesnake, or whichever band was in before you. There's all these gold discs everywhere – it's just not a very creative place to be, so we used to choose more neutral places.' By 'neutral', he meant Canned Applause came with no toilets, no running water and was located seven miles from the nearest town: 'It's got Nintendo, so that's all you need.' The nearest sign of life were the cows in the nearby field, which Thom disliked because 'they were near a power station, and were waiting to be incinerated, not a great vibe for recording.'

For a few weeks at Canned Applause the band did nothing but rehearse. Radiohead's work ethic is unquestionable and shames many other bands. In all, they rehearsed for four months before properly recording a single note. Each time they practised, they would tape the session and endlessly pore over the demo to see how they could improve. After this, they headed out to America and Canada for yet more gigs, and this five-week stint provided an invaluable opportunity to work on the new material. On their return, the band played a smattering of European festivals, including Glasgow's T in the Park again and headline show in Galway, Ireland.

When they returned to Canned Applause, Godrich had completed his work setting up the studio, and the band spent several more weeks recording early versions of the album tracks. Yet despite this painstaking approach, they were inspired by the speed at which they had recorded 'Lucky' for the *Help!* album, and planned on recording some of the new record in a similar fashion. However, it was nearly a whole year after starting when the album was completed, but three songs from these early sessions remained almost virtually unchanged on it: 'Subterranean Homesick Alien', 'Electioneering', and 'The Tourist', while a fourth track, 'No Surprises', was exactly the same version they recorded on the very first day of the Canned Applause sessions. What happened in the interim was that as the album unfolded, the speed slowed, it became more complex, and several songs passed through cluttered, complicated versions before the band decided that the more stripped-down initial take was preferable.

August saw them fly back out to America for twelve more dates supporting Alanis Morissette. The opportunity to play new material to tens of thousands of someone else's fans was again invaluable. On this tour, 'Paranoid Android' was over ten minutes long and included a bizarre lengthy organ climax in the place that the 'rain down' section, (so-called because of Thom's ethereal haunting vocals, would eventually occupy in the final version on the third album), where Jonny soloed like mad (he had increasingly played occasional keyboards during live shows) and Thom sang 'the walls . . . the walls' over and over. The band would often joke about the song at this stage, saying 'Ignore that. That was just a Pink Floyd cover.' Thom also said, 'There'd be little children crying at the end, begging their parents to take them home.' These dates gave them the chance to experiment: 'There was something about playing in really, really huge, sterile concrete structures,' Thom told *Jam Showbiz* , 'that was really important to the songs. Because a lot of the songs needed to sound quite big and messy and like they were bouncing off walls. When we went back into the studio, we were actually trying to create the sound of a shed soundcheck, or a big baseball stadium thing, without sounding like bloody Def Leppard or anything. Just the fact that you have this trashy, volatile thing going on around you, which we discovered was really important to the way we did the songs.'

Although the recording had initially progressed well, Nigel Godrich had watched with some concern – Canned Applause simply allowed the band too many distractions. They would all commute to and from home each day, and continued their social and private lives unaffected by the new record. Godrich was growing more concerned by the day that the band lacked focus, and on his suggestion, they decided to move wholesale to an even more remote location.

The one chosen was typically unusual – St Catherine's Court, a fifteenth-century country mansion, miles from anywhere in a secluded valley outside Bath, owned by the English Hollywood actress Jane Seymour. Complete with terraced gardens, a full-size ballroom and a bathroom filled with pictures of Ms Seymour in her underwear, the location was the perfect oasis. While she spent much of her life in Los Angeles, filming the hugely popular *Dr Quinn Medicine Woman* series, she rented her UK base out to corporations for conferences. Occasionally she had also hired it out to bands, most notably for Johnny Cash and then to the Cure for the recording of their commercially disastrous *Wild Mood Swings* album. Paying an enormous deposit in advance, Radiohead moved in. They never actually met her, but she did leave the keys and a note asking them to feed the cat.

After being intimidated at first by the eerie solitude and the huge house, the band were then rejuvenated by this isolated and distraction-free environment. They had month-long sessions there, in September and November 1996, rehearsing at home during October. Full use was made of the variety of unusual rooms in the mansion. Generally, they played in the ballroom, with Godrich recording them in the library. The superb vocals on 'Exit Music (For A Film)' were sung by Thom in the freezing cold stone-walled entrance hall.

Phil recorded many of his drum sections in the childrens' room, surrounded by cuddly toys (Colin joked that it looked like a cross between *Rock School* and *Blue Peter*!).

'It was like a dream workshop. We had all this gear, all these lights and lots of alcohol and food in this beautiful place.'

The band found that being so isolated meant they developed their own time frame, and often found themselves playing croquet in the middle of the night, then recording as dawn broke – in this way, 'Let Down' was completed at 3am in the ballroom. The experience was very intense, and they thought about nothing but the album during their stay there. 'It was like a dream workshop,' Thom told *Addicted To Noise*. 'We had all this gear, all these lights and lots of alcohol and food in this beautiful place. When it was working, it was the biggest fucking buzz I'd ever had, and when it wasn't, it was totally terrifying for me. It was like, "We spent all this time and all this money and, oh, my God, fuck!"' He also said, 'It became a complete fever, like being ill all the time. But looking at it in retrospect, most of the songs were done in four hours, and we really didn't change anything afterward. So I wonder what we were doing for a year?'

Thom was convinced the house was haunted, as he told *Spin*, 'The house was . . . oppressive. To begin with, it was curious about us. Then it got bored with us. And it started making things difficult. It started doing things like turning the studio tape machines on and off, rewinding them. Plus, it was in a valley on the outskirts of Bath, in the middle of nowhere. So when we actually stopped playing music there was just this pure silence. Open the window: nothing. A completely unnatural silence – not even birds singing. It was fucking horrible. I could never sleep.'

Despite this, the recordings produced some innovative and highly creative moments. The opening 'Airbag' took shape after Phil had been listening to some Mo Wax sounds; he then cut up his drum sounds then reconstituted it into the backing track. 'For two days, we did programming,' Ed told *Guitar World*, 'cutting up bits of drumming we had done and we didn't really know what we were doing. I think everybody thought we were mad. So to see the song actually come together . . . it was brilliant.' Thom was so pleased when they mixed it that

Radiohead had finally come to be acknowledged as one of the great bands of the nineties.

he ran out of the studio and phoned his girlfriend to tell her. As with most of their material, Phil gets to decide on the best take: 'Ultimately, Phil, our drummer, had the final say. He has to be happy with the drum take.'

'Paranoid Android', which would become the first single from the album, was a complicated affair, not least because of the three disparate yet cohesive sections. It had been inspired by a bad experience Thom had had one night in a Los Angeles bar. He had gone there for a quiet drink, but found himself surrounded by parasitic groupie types and pretentious California posers. Unbeknown to him, virtually everyone in the room, except himself, was on cocaine. 'The people I saw that night were just like demons from another planet,' he told *NME*. 'Everyone was trying to get something out of me. I felt like my own self was collapsing in the presence of it, but I also felt completely, utterly part of it, like it was all going to come crashing down any minute.' The band had been playing the song for months in rehearsals, but that night, while he couldn't sleep, the lyrics flooded into Thom's head at 5am. Of particular horror to him was one especially vicious lady who had a drink spilt over her dress and whose face contorted in venom at the culprit – she was the 'kicking, squealing Gucci little piggy' that Thom sang of and he was horrified. 'Basically it's just about chaos, chaos, utter fucking chaos.'

At first the band had hoped to record the entire track as one piece, but found this was too demanding – consequently, they recorded each part and then later spliced them together. When it was finished, they realised how good it was and decided to keep the rest of the album to that level, increasing the pressure on them still further.

'Climbing Up The Walls' dated back to the REM tour, and had first been played during a soundcheck at Hershey Stadium. 'Lucky' was the same version as on the *Help!* album – the band tried to re-record it but found they couldn't capture the same 'chaos' as in the original. 'Exit Music (For A Film)' was also an older track, and had originally been penned in to feature in the *Romeo & Juliet* film (which eventually went with 'Talk Show Host'). Once it was recorded, the band felt it was too good to just be on a soundtrack. 'Subterranean Homesick Alien' was initially written on an acoustic guitar, like many Radiohead songs, then Thom developed it on acoustic piano, but oddly enough, neither of these instruments were left on the final version.

Retro recording techniques were used – tape loops were employed at will rather than hi-tech samplers. The old-fashioned Mellotron, a relic of early synthesisers, was also wheeled into action. 'When it was used in the seventies people used to find dead mice inside it and it would stop working, it's that kind of level of technology.' Jonny produced a stunning array of weird sounds and atmospheres, often improvised, and Phil frequently treated his drum sounds with heavy reverb, echo or even guitar effects pedals.

'I think Thom at times has a hang-up about his voice. And the fucker can sing anything – he can reduce you to tears.'

Lyrically, Thom had a very definite agenda – to make each vocal totally different from the others ('he was getting sick of the fact he could sing about garden furniture and still sound very passionate'). He still felt insecure about his singing ability, despite the stunning work on *The Bends*, and this drove him to search for something extra. He claimed that his vocals were just an addendum to the music, that they were not central, but Ed totally disagreed, saying 'Vocals are the most important thing on a song – the music can be shite but be redeemed by a great vocal take, but Thom doesn't see it like that . . . I think Thom at times has a hang-up about his voice. And the fucker can sing anything – he can reduce you to tears.'

Thom was much influenced on this album by an incident that had happened way back when the band was still called On A Friday. A girlfriend of his had listened to an early demo and said, 'Your lyrics are crap. They're too honest, too personal, too direct and there's nothing left to the imagination'. Thom said that he agreed with her (although he was initially gutted), and then when he started to work with the rest of the band, he found that if he thought more about the lyrics they became less personal: 'I suddenly discovered that, if I did concentrate on the lyrics, I'd get much more out of writing and it would be easier to put a song together. Now we find that if we haven't got the lyrics to a song, we can't finish it because they dictate where we take the music.' This process was applied often in these recording sessions, with Thom completing many of the vocals on the first take. 'The Tourist' is an example: 'I don't remember doing it. It was something we left on the shelf for months. When I listened to it again it had obviously been, "Go out and sing a rough vocal so we can work on it." There's no emotional involvement in it . . . I'm just, "Yeah, yeah, sing the song and walk off."'

While they were deep in recording sessions, the band would often log on the Internet, scouring the dozens of web sites dedicated to themselves. Inspired by the detailed and highly informed work of the fans, the band decided to produce a site of their own. Instead of headlining Phoenix and Reading (they turned both down) they spent a week designing their web site, which gave limited free access to recordings as they evolved, as well as the latest news on the sessions' progress. They also proudly posted bad reviews, and admired rather than sued the carefully collated unofficial pages. Most strange of all, they logged on to the chat rooms to find people did not believe they were who they said they were. Jonny requested unusual chords from fans, but was sent nothing more sinister than a G Minor 7th. Thom unearthed even more useful ideas – he often visited sites to find pages filled with the new lyrics to the album, often for songs that he hadn't completed yet. Fans had taped concerts and tried to decipher his often difficult articulation from the bootleg. As a result, many of the lyrics were wildly wrong, but Thom found them enormously helpful – in some instances he actually lifted words from the web that were incorrect versions of lyrics he had been singing live.

'I used to shake people's hands and say, "I trust I can rely on your vote." They'd go "ha, ha, ha" and look at me like I was a nutcase.'

This desire to find new ideas applied to the music as well. Someone told them that Brian Eno had cards in his studio which said 'Whatever worked last time, never do it again.' They felt the weight of this edict, but were simultaneously inspired by it. They had a variety of other inspirations for the album. Will Hutton's *The State We're In*, a depressing account of Britain after years of Tory government, provided motivation for some of the ideas. As even more central influence was Miles Davis's 1970 jazz fusion double opus *Bitches Brew*. Jonny had plagued Thom to listen to this record for years, and when he finally did it made an indelible mark on his writing. Although musically there is very little common ground between the two records, the undertone of Davis' work inspired Thom immensely. 'The first time I heard it,' he told one journalist, 'I thought it was the most nauseating chaos, I felt sick listening to it. Then gradually something incredibly brutal about it and incredibly beautiful . . . It was at the core of what we were trying to do with [the new album].' 'Subterranean Homesick Alien' was born directly out of Thom listening to *Bitches Brew* night after night in his car.

Elvis Costello was again an influence for Thom, and the band have also acknowledged a debt to *The Prison Tapes* by Johnny Cash. Among the numerous other artists they credited as influential are Marvin Gaye, the Beach Boys (specifically *Pet Sounds*), and Kraftwerk and Bjork to a degree. They also drew heavily on books and writers, including the American professor Noam Chomsky. Thom ploughed through his collected works and especially loved the classic *Manufacturing Consent*, whose influence is seen in 'Electioneering'. 'I had this phase', he recalled in *Jam Showbiz*, 'I went through on an American tour where we just seemed to be shaking hands all the time, and I was getting a bit sick of it and upset by it. So I came up with this running joke with myself, where I used to shake people's hands and say, "I trust I can rely on your vote." They'd go "ha, ha, ha" and look at me like I was a nutcase.' His distaste for the 'music biz' was also reflected in the line 'riot sheelds, voodoo economicks, it's just business'. On a more jovial note, the band enjoyed the cartoon work of Magnus Carlsson during their heavier sessions. His chief character, Robin, provided light relief from the stress sessions, entertaining them with his mixture of naiveté, innocence and cunning.

They also admitted the impact of classical music on their new record. Tired of the standard rock arrangements of strings, which Jonny said hadn't changed much since the days of the Beatles and 'Eleanor Rigby', Radiohead instead looked to more unusual composers, in their own words, 'stealing a lot from the Polish composer Penderecki's string ideas . . . we've found all these composers that are still getting new sounds out of violins'. This can be heard on the last chord of 'Climbing Up The Walls', when a block of white noise is actually the sound of sixteen violins playing quarter tones from each other.

By Christmas 1996, the band had completed fourteen songs, with a dozen or so rougher ideas discarded. The New Year saw these tracks mixed and polished off in London. Only two songs from this batch didn't make it to the final album – 'Polyethelene' and 'A Reminder', which eventually appeared on the B-side of the album's first single, 'Paranoid Android'.

In typical Radiohead style, even the conclusion of the sessions provided dramatic. They had been working on the record for a year and there was no will

to complete it. However, Jonny had had enough and decided he had to take control. One day he walked in to the studio and told the band to stop. 'It wasn't quite that precious,' he explained to *Rolling Stone*. 'I didn't say, "That's it darling, my artistic juices are fully spent, I'm creatively drained," and throw the back of my hand to my forehead. It was more that I'd had enough, rather than I couldn't do any more . . . It's only 45–50 minutes of music, it was sounding great to my ears, we were just being nervous, being Radiohead.' Even then, Thom worried for weeks over the exact track order, playing the band dozens of versions of the running list. 'They didn't listen to any of them, 'cos they knew I'd fucking lost it.'

'When we realised what we had done, we had qualms about the fact that we had created this thing that was quite revolting.'

The album's monicker was originally 'a bad song with a good title', which gradually became a mantra for the sessions: 'We would walk around the studio like robots going, "OK, Computer!" And it kind of stuck.' With the album finally in the bag, they were reluctant to hint in public at what was coming. All that Thom would say was 'I don't think it's quite as people imagined it would be.' A few weeks later, when listening to the record with some objectivity, Thom was startled to hear what they had created: 'When we realised what we had done, we had qualms about the fact that we had created this thing that was quite revolting.'

• • •

The first taste of the forthcoming behemoth was the release of the single 'Paranoid Android', in May 1997. The near seven-minute epic, with its diversity and range of sounds, from acoustic lament to virtual white noise, was perhaps the least obvious single to make from the album. Allegedly, when the BBC Radio 1 programmer (desperate at last to join in the growing fanfare for the band) first heard it, he needed to sit down afterwards. Perhaps he had heard Thom's bizarre lyrics, which included the line 'I'm tryin' to get some rest, from all the unborn chicken voices in my head.'

Previous pages: The recording sessions for Radiohead's third album, OK Computer.

The obvious analogy to make was to call the track 'the Bohemian Rhapsody for the nineties', but the band denied this. Ed: 'It's not – it's just a handy reference point. It's like 'Creep' was meant to sound like Scott Walker. But "Paranoid Android" is the song we play to people when they want to know what the album's like, 'cos it should make them think, "What the fuck is going to happen on the rest of the album?"' The band were disappointed that most people missed the humour in this release: 'A lot of it makes us laugh. "Paranoid Android" makes me laugh. It's cheeky, it's tongue in cheek. It's the track we were most proud of and we wanted people to come and smirk at it, too.'

The video for the single was equally controversial. It was a cartoon by their admired Magnus Carlsson (who had almost no experience of pop promos) which was based on the cartoon character that Radiohead loved so much, Robin and his friend Benji. The band did not send Magnus any lyrics, so he just sat in his garden, listening to the song over and over, whilst writing down the pictures that came into his head. Carlsson found it quite easy: 'The good thing about the song is that it's very filmic in structure,' he said in *Promo Magazine*, 'There are three or four different songs there, more or less, with different tempos and different characters.' The promo depicted fish with human breasts, people being sliced up, mice copulating, leather-clad men and some S&M imagery – complete with a fleeting set of Radiohead caricatures, sitting around a table watching a man with a head growing out of his stomach strip in front of them. MTV deemed it necessary to censor the nipples in the video, but oddly decided that the part where a man saws through his own limbs was acceptable. Suitably altered, the video was placed on immediate high rotation in their 'Buzz Bin'. One part shows a drink being spilt over someone, which was a pure coincidence – Magnus had no idea that was exactly the same event that had inspired Thom to write the lyrics to the song one night in Los Angeles.

Radiohead had originally planned to film a video for every track off the album, with a possible cinema release, but the sheer financial and time restraints soon quashed the idea. A promo was made for 'Let Down', but it was scrapped, in the process wasting $100,000, half of which the band had to pay.

• • •

OK Computer opened with the especially complex, rhythmic, claustrophobic 'Airbag'. It was originally titled 'Last Night An Airbag Saved My Life,' after the 1983 disco hit by Indeep, 'Last Night A DJ Saved My Life'. Characterised by odd tremolo guitar courtesy of Jonny, the track is chockfull of offbeat melodies, loops and evocative pseudo-eastern leads. However, in many ways, this was Phil's track, with his cut up drum patterns indicative of the influence of drum and bass and musicians like DJ Shadow ('Paranoid Android' was also partly inspired by this revered musician). Thom sings of being 'back to save the universe', while Colin's funky bass makes this the album's most danceable track. It reinforces Thom's apparent obsession with cars, something that had been a feature of many Radiohead songs, and which stems from a potentially fatal near-miss he had in a car with his girlfriend when he was just seventeen. Ed told one magazine it was 'about the wonderful, positive emotion you feel when you've just failed to have an accident; when you just miss someone and realise how close it was and stop the car and just feel this incredible elation. There's something joyous about it – life suddenly seems more precious.'

When the single 'Paranoid Android' kicks in, with it symphonic structure and huge diversity of rhythm and sound, it is already crystal clear that this is no ordinary album. Gentle acoustic arpeggios and assorted clickings and shufflings initially remind the listener of *The Bends*, but that soon changes when the clashing, menacing guitars drop in and the song goes mental. Complicated tempo changes, atonal touches and flashes of dissonance further muddy the waters, but the band never get lost in self-indulgence. It has King Crimson-style melodies that are protracted but compelling, and Thom's lyrics, which he said were 'actually polaroids inside my head', are vitriolic and neurotic – 'the crackle of pig skin, the yuppies networking/the vomit, the vomit, god loves his children yeah!' They somehow manage to draw the line between pomp and pop, and the result is daringly executed. The highlight is the chilling, other-worldly 'rain down' section.

'I believe that there are little ones [aliens] who are buried underground, waiting to surface. I just wanna be visited. I wanna see 'em. I wanna see ghosts. I want to know.'

The next song, whose title is a tribute to Bob Dylan, 'Subterranean Homesick Alien', brings Thom's vocal to the fore, gentle and lilting. It talks of a longing to be abducted by aliens, of aliens filming home movies for their folks back home, of dark country lanes and spaceships. On the surface, the subject matter could have been laughably pretentious or downright ludicrous, but the sensuous instrumentation and skillful production layer the track with too much sprawling musical curiosity to fall into that trap. Thom made it quite clear the extra-terrestrial hankering in the song was not fictional: 'I believe that there are little ones [aliens] who are buried underground, waiting to surface. I just wanna be visited. I wanna see 'em. I wanna see ghosts. I want to know.' The song was inspired by Thom mowing down a pheasant in a country lane. The darkness, the silence and the event itself all stirred up his emotions and produced this blistering song, including the words 'take me on board their beautiful ship, show me the world as I'd love to see it.' It reminded him of earlier days: 'When I was a kid at school one of the very first essays I had to do was this essay that asked, "If you were an alien landing from another planet, how would you describe what you saw?" I just thought, "That's a really mind-blowing question."' He also said, 'I'm like most people; I'd love to be abducted. Then they'd have something for the rest of their lives. It's the ultimate madness.'

'Exit Music (For A Film)' was the first time the band had written a song on demand, for Baz Luhrmann's aforementioned 1996 hyperkinetic version of *Romeo and Juliet*. Initially, Thom had tried to include lines from the play itself, but that soon proved too cumbersome. The band were sent the last half hour of the film while they were touring with Alanis Morissette, and wrote their track to that. In the closing scenes of the film, Juliet holds a Colt 45 to her head, which particularly disturbed Thom – he thus sings, 'Pack and get dressed, before your father hears us, before all hell breaks loose'. Gentle strumming again opens the chilling song, which ideally captures the passion and innocence of the play itself. One of the album's harder tracks to listen to, it is nevertheless an uncomfortable yet brilliant song, underpinned by a brutal bass line which almost pounds the gentler refrains of the song into submission. Once again, Thom's haunting voice is crammed full with emotion, drawing the listener in completely. They used the Mellotron for the voices, and thereafter the song was completed in two days.

'Let Down' is perhaps the strongest connection between earlier albums and *OK Computer*, possibly the only track that can justify comparisons to stadium rock or U2's Bono. The chiming, Byrds-like guitars make it one of the album's most melodic tracks, but again the dour lyrical turns and Thom's pained vocals roughen the edges – 'crushed like a bug in the ground, let down and hanging around'. It is about loss of control, sadness and anger. Thom was at his most visual in these lyrics, comparing himself to helpless crushed bugs, utterly useless. As he told *Humo*, 'Andy Warhol once said that he could enjoy his own boredom. "Let down" is about that. It's the transit-zone feeling. You're in a space, you are collecting all these impressions, but it all seems so vacant. You don't have control over the earth anymore. You feel very distant from all these thousands of people that are also walking there.' The track is beautifully melancholic, with its guitar crescendo churning the emotions.

While the band were touring in 1996, they had a catchphrase that helped them ignore particularly nasty people – 'the karma police will catch up with him sooner or later'. The phrase gave the title of 'Karma Police', which was to be the album's second single. It manages to avoid the naff use of the word as happened in the late sixties and early seventies, and use it in a dark and almost Orwellian vision. It is, in a sense, the most conventional song on the album, but is certainly not lightweight. The piano-driven hooks, and beautifully weary yet straight rhythms gave it a vitality and brevity, playfully reminiscent of XTC. Of the central tenet of the song, Thom explained 'Karma is important. The idea that something like karma exists makes me happy. It makes me smile. I get more sympathetical. "Karma Police" is dedicated to everyone who works for a big firm. It's a song against bosses.' Thom sings, 'Karma police arrest this girl, her hitler hairdo is making me feel ill,' summing up a hated, meglomaniacal work colleague who is all too familiar to anyone who has worked for vicious superiors. The track obviously struck a chord as on its release as a single it reached number 8 in August 1997.

The album's strangest track, and one which would inevitably incite heavy use of the skip button on the stereo, was the bizarre, Eno-esque 'Fitter Happier'. Eerie piano ramblings and violin screechings provide the backdrop to a Macintosh-synthesised voice (called Fred, not the scientist Stephen Hawking, as some people thought) listing a two-minute litany of platitudes to aim for in a perfect modern life – advert slogans, media myths, lifestyle ideals and so on. Thom had been reading various self-help books and making these lists and they somehow transformed into a song. Thom later said, 'The computer was the most emotional voice I had ever heard, at the time.'

Surprisingly, Thom already disowned the lyrics by the time the album was released: 'I'm not standing behind the lyrics any more. Sometimes your ideas get entangled with other ideas and then you have to apologise for the original idea because it doesn't make sense any more. That's what happened with 'Fitter Happier'. Now, I listen to the piano part.' At one point, they considered putting this track as the opener, but decided against it, as it would have been 'right over the boundaries of what's decent'.

The album's most searing rock track was next, 'Electioneering', also the record's most directly political effort. Thom has said in the past that the endless promotional stints he undertook made him feel like a campaigning politician, 'kissing babies, shaking hands'. To add to this feeling, his distaste for multi-nationals and corporations is expressed in uncomfortable guitars and abrasive sounds. This track is a good example of how Thom was more objective on this album – 'The songs are far less personal than the ones on *The Bends*. I didn't feel that same need to tell my own story. I was much more involved in other peoples worlds, and I put my own thoughts in perspective.' Ed was a little more humorous, saying 'If Tony Blair can behave as a pop-star, why shouldn't we feel a bit like politicians?' It is in the process, possibly Radiohead's most difficult ever song.

The atmosphere is brought back down again with the superb 'Climbing Up The Walls', a truly disturbing song from within the mind of a serial killer. Thom sounds utterly demented throughout, the atmosphere created by the three guitars and the quirky noises is frightening, and the overall effect is truly magnificent. It is a mountain of chaos from start to finish, quite horrible, quite brilliant – 'I am the pick in the ice, do not cry out or hit the alarm, we are friends till we die,' sings Thom as the evil killer. Thom was clearly heavily involved in the song, telling the media 'Was it an accident that of the ten largest mass-murderers in Americas history, eight have occurred since 1980, typically acts of middle-aged white men in their thirties and forties after a prolonged period of being lonely, frustrated and full of rage and precipitated by a catastrophe in their lives such as losing their jobs or divorce?' He also said, less cryptically, 'Some people don't dare to sleep with the window open, because they're afraid that the monsters that they see in their imagination will come inside. This song is about the monster in the closet.' It is an album highpoint, a pivotal moment.

This terrifying track is followed by the record's softest lament, the simply beautiful 'No Surprises', a glockenspiel-led nursery rhyme about suicide. It is on the one-hand the album's most commercial, stadium friendly song, and yet also one that is totally inappropriate to the cigarette-lighters-aloft status that it will inevitably attract. Shaking hands with carbon monoxide is hardly the stuff of

'I find landfills really curious. All this stuff is getting buried, the debris of our lives. It doesn't rot, it just stays there.'

Top of the Pops, but the song's beauty secured it entry at number 2 when it was finally released in January 1998. The band claimed it was a vain attempt to re-write Louis Armstrong's 'What A Wonderful World'. The gorgeous track is Thom's own, his voice is staggering and the sentiment shatteringly sad – the opening couplet is 'a heart that's full up like a landfill, a job that slowly kills you, bruises that won't heal'. The rest of the band were astonished when they first heard this track: 'On this album, the lyrics opened me up to stuff that I hadn't necessarily noticed before or maybe felt,' Ed told *Addicted To Noise*, 'but couldn't put into words. And I think it's amazing that he can do that. "No Surprises" just floored me.' Thom shied away from the obvious 'suicidal maniac' accusations by saying '[It's a] fucked-up nursery rhyme. A desperate bid to try and get back to normalcy and failing miserably. It stems from my unhealthy obsession of what to do with plastic boxes and plastic bottles. You can't throw them all away. Then I got into landfills and general household things. I find landfills really curious. All this stuff is getting buried, the debris of our lives. It doesn't rot, it just stays there. That's how we deal, that's how I deal with stuff, I bury it.'

The excellent, expansive and epic 'Lucky' came next, included to make up for the embarrassment of only charting at number 51 on its single release. At the time, the band claimed it was the best song they had ever done, and was created 'because we're so bad at covers. Always have been even when we were a school band we couldn't do them.' Closing what was an awesome journey was 'The Tourist', with music written entirely by Jonny, who expressed surprise when the band allowed it on the album. It is the calming down, with minimal vocals, mellow guitars and monastic chants. Of this piece he said, 'We just wanted a song where we weren't paranoid about making something happen every three seconds and where we could record it with space.' Thom wrote the lyrics while on holiday in Prague, where he spliced random notes and words together into a compelling montage. With its warnings to slow down, the song effectively brings us back to the car-centric opening blast of 'Airbag'. It is the perfect finale to one of *the* great albums.

< chapter: 9 >

I'M YOUR SUPERHERO, WE ARE STANDING ON THE EDGE

The critical response to *OK Computer* was frenzied. The dictionary was emptied of its superlatives as almost universal acclaim flooded in. *Rolling Stone* hailed it as evidence that they were 'one rock band still willing to look the devil square in the eyes'. *Q* magazine said, 'Now Radiohead can definitely be ranked high among the world's great bands.' *Select* called it 'A landslide victory', while another journalist said it was 'Radiohead's most epic, sensitive, inventive and ultimately compelling outing yet' (although it should be noted the band failed to win a Brit award again, and didn't even attend the ceremony this time).

Lofty comparisons were frequent, from REM's *New Adventures In Hi-Fi*, to King Crimson, Pink Floyd and even Genesis. The on-line magazine *Addicted To Noise* claimed, wrongly, that it was inspired by Philip K. Dick's monumental book *Valis*, even though Thom stated he had never read it. The chart success of the singles from the project, 'Paranoid Android', 'Karma Police' and 'No Surprises', added to the album's hefty achievement. All this praise made Thom uncomfortable. He believed that in the last analysis these were self-perpetuating people trying to out-do each other with compliments. This unsettled him: 'There are two difficult words that are always coming back in the reviews: "escapistic" and "epic". I don't think we are escapistic. And epic? I don't know. An epic album is something for background music. If you put on *OK Computer* in a trendy bar, all those trendy posers will choke in their own goatees.' He was disappointed that people assumed the lyrics were personal, when he had in fact made it clear that on this record he had looked outside of himself for the first time (encouraged in part by talks with Michael Stipe). However, Jonny felt that Thom was fooling himself a little, and that there was still a large element of autobiography in there: 'He confesses. He'd never admit that though. It's just like Mark E. Smith pretending none of his songs are about himself.' Thom was also bemused by the claims of inaccessibility, with the general consensus being that the album needed a dozen listens before it could be partly understood: 'I never got inaccessible. It was a fucking pop record. That's it. That's what we do.'

The album's chart topping success in the UK dragged their previous two albums back into the Top 40. Meanwhile across the Atlantic, its success was rather more modest. In the USA the album charted at number 21, the same week that techno-monsters Prodigy entered straight at number 1, thus beginning their summertime conquest of the States. Capitol had initially loved the sound of the live material when Radiohead were touring with Alanis, but were then

'We're not interested in saving rock. It should have been dead years ago.'

disappointed when they heard the finished tapes for *OK Computer*, and realised it had transformed into something altogether more sinister and darker than the stadium album they were hoping for. Manager Chris Hufford said they were undeterred by this reaction: 'By that time the UK had grabbed it and said, "This is fucking awesome!" So we steamed in and said to America, "Get your industry heads off, forget the bloody singles, just listen to it like a punter for a few weeks and you'll realise what an amazing piece of work this is." Thankfully, that's what happened. They started saying, "You're right, this is amazing, but now what the fuck do we do with it?!"'

With Capitol President Gary Gersh now saying, 'We won't let up until they are the biggest band in the world,' Aiwa personal stereos, which had the album glued into the casing so that recipients had to listen, were sent out to the press. As the band's UK reputation spilled over into the US, American critical response was as positive as the British; in addition, there was a general feeling that, in the light of recent relatively disappointing sales for U2 and REM, modern rock could do with a 'saviour'. *Rolling Stone* loved the album, the *Los Angeles Times* included it in their Top Ten of the year and other influential magazines like *Spin*, *Alternative Press* and *Details* all hailed it as a great work. It later won the band a Grammy award for Best Alternative Act. At a concert in Irving Plaza in New York to open their album dates in the US, celebrities in attendance included Madonna, Michael Stipe, Bono, Courtney Love, Lenny Kravitz, Marilyn Manson, Sheryl Crow, Noel and Liam Gallagher, and dozens of supermodels. Only the lack of substantial radio play meant the album's progress stalled somewhat, but the band's profile had been raised enormously. All the same, Thom was uneasy, saying, 'To have all this hype around the record is not something I've ever had to deal with . . . a lot of the hype is being shouldered by me. I'm not into it at all.' As for being rock's saviour he was even more dismissive, saying, 'We're not interested in saving rock. It should have been dead years ago.'

The band were taken aback by the volume and depth of the reviewers' praise. Although they were surprised people called it difficult, they were delighted that its many layers seemed to have been noticed, as Thom told *Select*: 'I was really amazed about the way the people described how it sounded as well . . . like the sound of Ed's guitar on the beginning of "No Surprises" or the way "Airbag" starts . . . and for people to pick up on those things was a real fucking kick. Really cool.'

'I think people feel sick when they hear *OK Computer*. Nausea was part of what we were trying to create.'

The band themselves were delighted at the album. '*OK Computer* is like buying a polaroid camera, getting on a high-speed train and taking lots of photos of what's going on, going past. So that's how it is for me. I like that.' Thom also acknowledged the abrasive nature of the record, saying, 'I think people feel sick when they hear *OK Computer*. Nausea was part of what we were trying to create.'

The only real criticism of *OK Computer* was that it was redolent of that great seventies monster, 'prog-rock', which conjured up images of flared trousers, pompous album artwork, soloist self-indulgence and gargantuan synthesisers. With its enormous scope, its artwork, and its dense subject matter, critics were quick to suggest Radiohead were drifting into prog rock territory. The band did not help matters, saying things like the title 'refers to embracing the future, it refers to being terrified of the future, of our future, of everybody else's. It's to do with standing in a room where all these appliances are going off and all these machines and computers and so on, they are all going off and the sound it makes.'

Nevertheless, this analysis was wide of the mark. The six minute 'Paranoid Android' was cited as an example, but Oasis's 'All Around The World' is over nine minutes long and you don't hear them compared to Emerson, Lake and Palmer. The much-vaunted theory that the album was a concept piece about the age-old fear of the mechanised world being dehumanised by computers and technology was something the band themselves had not envisaged. Despite *Rolling Stone* calling it 'a stunning art-rock tour de force', the band totally disagreed. 'Oh God,' a horrified Colin said, 'What a ghastly thought. That makes it sound like Rick Wakeman and his Knights of the Round Table On Ice.' Jonny thought it was merely a case of the media thinking to much: 'I think one album title and one computer voice do not make a concept album. That's a bit of a red herring.'

Besides, as Thom said, Radiohead had very simple motives: 'We write pop songs. As time has gone on, we've gotten more into pushing our material as far as it can go. But there was no intention of it being "art". It's a reflection of all the disparate things we were listening to when we recorded it.' As one isolated critic pointed out, Radiohead in fact still owed their existence to punk bands like Magazine, they took from REM, Nirvana, and even jazz. Rifling through their record collections would always reveal far more of these bands than Genesis, Yes and Emmerson, Lake and Palmer. Indeed, Jonny spent much of 1996 listening to Ennio Moricone and classical albums. Thom was perhaps most succinct in their dismissal of this popular 'prog-rock' theory: 'They're talking bollocks.'

At a time when Prodigy reigned supreme in America, alongside the Spice Girls on top of the pop world, British alternative music was flourishing. Primal Scream were back, the Charlatans and Shaun Ryder's Black Grape were holding the light aloft for Manchester, while fellow Mancunians Oasis were still enormous. Despite this substantial competition, *OK Computer* was undoubtedly the album of 1997, and has already rightly been listed in history's list of watershed records.

The world tour for *OK Computer* was typically lengthy, with Radiohead maintaining their hard work ethic in covering as many territories as possible. This period had been their longest time away from the stage since signing their record deal, so they were understandably nervous. Having kicked off in Barcelona on 22 May, the band's first airing of the new record in the UK was at an epochal Glastonbury headline slot in late June. Before that they played more overseas dates, including one in San Diego, where Thom walked in on the aggressive rockers Insane Clown Posse, who are never seen in public without their make-up. He entered just as they were applying their face-masks, so they jumped up, threw him against the wall, and told him in no uncertain terms what would happen if he ever did that again.

When the band arrived back in the UK, they were tired and listless, so the dates which should have been a homecoming were rather jaded, in particular a gig at the Brixton Academy, which Thom said he 'hated'. He did, however, enjoy a fan-club-only date at London's Astoria, despite having been up all the previous night with food poisoning. At the show, members of the fan club, Wasted, witnessed a superb, unself-conscious gig, including a section of obscure B-sides. They also played a highly secret home-town gig at the tiny Zodiac, the popular Oxford club which they had bought shares in after the success of *The Bends*. Other key dates this year included a performance on the *Tonight Show* With Jay Leno to open the US tour, and a performance at the hugely successful Tibetan Freedom Concert on Randall's Island, New York, organised by The Beastie Boys, alongside, U2, Blur, Bjork and the Foo Fighters.

Their biggest slot of their own tour came on 22 June at the massive Dublin RDS with Massive Attack in support. The 33,000 tickets were sold out in a few hours and with such high expectations, the band found themselves very on edge, as Thom told Rolling Stone: 'It was sheer blind terror. My most distinctive memory of the whole year was the dream I had that night: I was running down the [River] Liffey, stark bollock naked, being pursued by a huge tidal wave.'

Most gigs on the tour were opened by the droning voice from 'Fitter, Happier' before the band launched into 'Airbag'. Previous touring experience, and an impressive back catalogue, meant that Radiohead were now an awesome force live. While Thom was the obvious focal point, Jonny's multi-instrumental skills made him an ideal accomplice – the glockenspiel he gently struck on 'No Surprises', or the radio he tuned in at random on 'Climbing Up The Walls', were pleasant diversions he could engage in because of his assured and brilliant guitar work each night. Thom, meanwhile, was brimming with confidence at last, and when they played 'Creep' he often introduced it by saying, 'Here's some karaoke nonsense for the indie fans' before changing the lyrics from 'I'm a weirdo' to 'I'm a winner'.

The key gig of the tour, however, was unquestionably the aforementioned headline slot at the Glastonbury Festival. Despite a pathetic threat from the tiresome and stale Ocean Colour Scene to blow Radiohead off stage, this festival was the peak of the band's career. Although they were veterans of years of hard gigging, the scale of the headline slot (which their agent had been negotiating for over a year), did not escape them, and their nerves were suitably frayed on the day – 'We were running on pure blind terror when we went on.' Unfortunately, things started to go wrong soon after they started playing. The opening two songs were brilliant, but then Thom's monitor speakers blew up. Subsequently the lighting faltered, so that the band were faced with a retina-burning barrage of naked light. At this stage, the on-stage sound was atrocious and they couldn't even see the audience. 'Talk Show Host' clattered to a premature and broken end. The whole event was threatening to go horribly wrong, and Thom would have killed the PA man if he had seen him. He later remembered thinking, 'Thanks very much for fucking my life up in front of all these people. I remember "Paranoid Android" starting up. I couldn't hear anything . . . having to sing to that. In front of 40,000 people.'

Then something amazing happened. They turned the lights on the 40,000 people out there watching them, and Thom noticed that they were loving it. In an instant, the show was transformed. Despite standing knee deep in mud, after being rained on for the entire weekend, the festival goers were transfixed. Radiohead had refused to be beaten: 'It was the most important hour and a half of our lives,' Thom later told *Select*, 'and no fucker was going to take it away from us. There was a point where I did walk off, but I turned back. And then the fireworks went off. Literally. It was bonkers.'

After the gig, it was clear that those present had seen a performance that would go down in rock history. Even the band acknowledge this, with Thom continuing, 'The best thing about that is the way that people come up to us now

'There was a point where I did walk off, but I turned back. And then the fireworks went off. Literally. It was bonkers.'

and say, "I was at Glastonbury." There was a friend of mine who's seen us a million times, ever since we started. And he was up in the hills, stoned out of his

face with all these old people in tents that he didn't really know, and he said everyone was turning around saying, "This is where we're all at, right now." *Apocalypse Now.* It was *Apocalypse Now.*' Thom said, 'It was the best day of my life and the worst day of my life. Without doubt.' Charlie Myatt, their agent, was a little more unequivocal, saying, 'I thought it must be like me seeing Queen doing "Bohemian Rhapsody" in 1975 – a bit of history.'

'Whichever way we go, we'll go to an extreme, either loads of samplers or we'll strip it back down. The next album will probably be a bit of both.'

With the world tour for *OK Computer* keeping them on the road for the first part of 1998, Thom started writing new material in the back of the bus again. Nigel Godrich was flown out for all of their *OK Computer* dates in Europe, where [substantial quantities of] some new material was recorded while they were on the road. Hints were made of an early release of an EP or an album, but with Radiohead's recording history, the follow-up to *OK Computer* was not likely to surface for some time.

But while the acclaim for *OK Computer* was gathering momentum, Radiohead played yet more live dates around the world, touring Japan and Australasia, before heading to the States for their most eagerly anticipated shows across the Atlantic yet. Despite the album failing to reach the Billboard Top 10, there was a definite sense that the band's fanbase was growing ever stronger in America: all of these shows were sold out even before the band landed in the US for the first date at Theater Bayou Place in Houston, Texas.

The band appeared tired at many of the dates, and indeed actually apologised for being exhausted at the final New York gigs. Thom said 'Talk Show Host' was about being tired of touring, and then the final night of the tour declared the band's happiness to have finished their world tour at last. Other events kept them in good spirits. In February *Ok Computer* had won them a Grammy Award for Best Alternative Music Performance and it would not be their only accolade that spring. *Spin* magazine voted the band the second most vital artists in rock and at the Ivor Novello Awards in London for they triumphed in the categories of Best Contemporary Song (for 'Paranoid Android') and Best Song Musically and Lyrically (for 'Karma Police').

New material was very limited on these dates, with only two songs being debuted, namely 'Big Ideas (Don't Get Any)', also known as 'Nude', and 'How To Disappear Completely And Not Be Found'. Much to the chagrin of the more recent Radiohead converts in the crowd, the band also played many B sides, purely to keep themselves interested, including 'Talk Show Host', 'The Trickster', and 'Banana Co.' Notably, 'Creep' was never aired once. Also, the band re-learned 'Man-O-War', to appease the dozens of fans who asked them to play it every night. In April, during the tour, they released an EP titled 'Airbag/How Am I Driving?' which was intended as a mini-album to build on their American success but was also available on import in the UK. Unfortunately for dedicated fans the only new material on offer was the splendid packaging as the songs had all been previously released as B-sides to *Ok Computer*'s singles.

The dates themselves were largely incident-free, with a smattering of celebrities backstage, including Michael Stipe at San Francisco, and Thom occasionally forgetting the words to songs, and having to be helped out by the audience. There was also news of a threatened lawsuit from a band called Army Of Lovers, who were allegedly claiming that one of Radiohead's songs (probably 'Exit Music') bore striking similarities to their own track 'Crucified'.

Incident-free that is, except for a superb April Fool's joke that was played by the influential Los Angeles radio station KROQ. Thom was mooted as appearing on a breakfast show along with two DJs named Kevin and Bean. Before the singer arrived in the studio booth, the hosts of the show began making personal jibes about Thom's lazy eye, such as saying, 'The cool thing about interviewing Thom is that he can look at us both while answering the questions.' Then Thom apparently arrived, but that did little to stop the two from continuing their abuse. At first, Thom was in good humour and chuckled mildly at their rather tasteless cracks about his physical appearance – he even tried to explain how it had led him to be bullied as a child and the effect that this had on him in his later life: 'children can be cruel about these things – and so can radio personalities, I guess'. The DJs ignored this point, however, and continued to provoke the singer.

With no end in sight, Thom began to lose his patience. Fortunately, there was a respite when the DJs asked him to play an acoustic version of 'Fake Plastic Trees', and he went on to talk about the forthcoming collaboration with Drugstore, entitled 'El Presidente' (in which Thom was rumoured to appear naked in the video, a revelation for Radiohead fans that never actually materialised). Then to Thom's dismay they insisted he played 'Creep'. After finally relenting he was half way through playing the track when one of the DJs said, 'The interesting thing to watch when he plays that song, he's got one eye on the guitar . . .' Thom stopped dead, and it sounded as if he had walked out of the studio. Then, suddenly, the sounds of a violent struggle could be heard and screams and shouts rang out over the stunned airwaves. There was even the voice of a fan shouting, 'Don't hurt Thom – don't touch his face!'

The on-air brawl was punctuated with Thom shouting phrases such as 'It isn't so funny now, is it, mate?' before the programmers cut to a commercial break and then played several songs in a row. Afterwards, the DJs claimed that Thom had been sent to St. Josephs Medical Center in Burbank to have an X-ray on a punch he received to the head which might have caused possible eye damage. They told concerned listeners that although Thom hadn't spoken since, the show at the Universal Ampitheater was still scheduled.

The following day, the story rumbled on. Reporters came from the hospital to find out more information, and the DJs repeatedly apologised on air for the scuffle. There was even an interview with a supposed member of staff at the hospital who had taken Thom's X-ray. In the furore, over 1000 angry and concerned Radiohead fans besieged the station's switchboard, as well as the ticket office of the venue.

The first sign that the interview was a set-up came when Capitol Records denied that the band had been involved in any way. Then several listeners had pointed out on a frenzied Internet response to the fight that the acoustic songs Thom had played sounded remarkably similar to the versions recorded back in 1993 and 1995 for a show on KROQ. Finally, a few days later, the radio station admitted it was all an April Fool's joke. Thom had been played, very convincingly, by an impersonator called Ralph Garman, and the band were not involved on any level. Still, it generated more publicity than all of their hard-earned reviews put together!

By 20 April, Radiohead's main touring for the year was over. At the end of the month they released a compilation of their promotional videos, called *7 Television Commercials*, featuring the clips used for 'Paranoid Android', 'Street

Thom at the 1999 Tibetan Freedom Concert.

spirit', 'No Surprises', 'Just', 'High And Dry, 'Karma Police', and 'Fake Plastic Trees.' Before they finally relaxed, however, they first recorded a track, 'Big Boots' (the new title for 'Man-O-War'), for the forthcoming *Avengers* film; although they reserved the right to remove it from the soundtrack if they were unhappy with the finished song. Sure enough, the band later pulled the track. Thom explained why to Matt Pinfield of MTV: '. . . it was all a bit weird . . . I mean we went in and tried to do this old track that we had . . . and it just wasn't happening at all. It was a real low point after it.'

An area of activity that grew after the release of *OK Computer* was working with other musicians. In late 1997 Thom recorded a track in two days in San Francisco with DJ Shadow, once called 'the Jimmy Page of the sampler'. Intended for inclusion in James Lavelle's U.N.K.L.E project, the track, 'Rabbit In Your Headlights', was largely improvised. It appeared on the album *Psyence Fiction* which was released by Lavelle's MoWax Records in August 1998 and the track would subsequently become the first single from it. Most reviews agreed that 'Rabbit In Your Headlights' was one the finer moments on an album that failed to live up to it's hype and the accompanying video was both visually stunning and disturbing as it featured an odd-looking character being knocked down by a series of cars. MTV were particularly impressed, nominating it for Best Breakthrough Video at their 1999 Video Music Awards. However, the track's bleak nature meant it received little radio play, not affecting the chart position however since the single was too long to be eligible anyway.

> ## 'It was all a bit weird . . . I mean we went in and tried to do this old track that we had . . . and it ju wasn't happening at all. It was a real low point afte

Thom then contributed to the soundtrack for the film *Velvet Goldmine*, produced by Michael Stipe. For the highly stylised glam rock movie Thom and Jonny worked with Stipe himself as well as ex-Suede guitarist Bernard Butler, Tindersticks' Stuart Staples, and Roxy Music's Andy Mackay on three Roxy Music covers, 'ZHB', 'Ladytron' and 'Bittersweet'. Thom's collaboration with Drugstore on the 'El Presidente' single reached number 20 in the UK in April 1998 and was also featured on their album *White Magic For Lovers*.

The band then reported in as being officially on holiday, with the exception of the Tibetan Freedom Concert at the RFK Stadium in Washington DC on 13 and 14 June. Radiohead were scheduled to play on the first day along with Tracy Chapman, Sonic Youth, REM and Beck. Radiohead had had the Free Tibet movement's logo hanging on a banner from their keyboards throughout their tour, and despite threats from the Chinese authorities that their records would be banned in that country, along with anyone else appearing at the concert, Radiohead repeatedly told their audiences how much they were looking forward to playing the show. Yet again, however, things did not go to plan. A few hours before the concert started, torrential rain lashed Washington, and further dangerous weather conditions were predicted for later that day.

Initially, it seemed as if the warnings were exaggerated. There was blazing sunshine for the first couple of hours of the concert, and Money Mark, Mutabaruka, Live, the Dave Matthews band and KRS-One played the giant twin stages. Then, during Herbie Hancock and the Headhunters 25th anniversary reunion set, heavy rain began to fall. Suddenly, a bolt of lightning hit the crowd, injuring several fans, two of them seriously. The show quickly ground to a halt and an hour later at 3.40pm Michael Stipe went on stage to announce that the rest of that day's concert had been cancelled.

Radiohead did their best not to let their fans down, however, playing a surprise gig for the first 800 people who turned up with Saturday's ticket stubs at the nearby 9.30 club. Michael Stipe joined the band on 'Lucky' to sing lead vocals.

Fortunately, Radiohead were able to play the next day of the concert, along with all of the other cancelled acts except for Beck and Tracy Chapman. But Sunday had its problems, too. This time the weather was fine but equipment failures marred many of the sets, including those of Sean Lennon, Pulp and Sonic Youth. Radiohead, however, were unaffected by these technical gremlins and played a brilliant set, including 'Karma Police', 'Street Spirit (Fade Out)' and 'Lucky', which Michael Stipe sang again. For the first time that day the audience began to enjoy themselves, a mood undoubtedly heightened by the band's remarkable decision to play an extended version of 'Creep'. On stage Thom expressed the feelings of everyone when he said, 'This is more like it. This is a good day.'

Later Thom returned the favour to Michael Stipe for his singing 'Lucky' by joining REM during their set and singing 'Be Mine'. He also provided Patti Smith's part in 'E-bow the Letter' (the same extreme weather that had brought the previous day's concert to a close had stranded her at New York's LaGuardia airport.)

Back in Britain rumours circulated that Radiohead were to make a surprise appearance at Glastonbury, whispers reinforced by the sight of a band called On A Friday on the bill for Saturday night. These rumours proved unfounded but organiser Michael Eavis [has] enthusiastically suggested that Radiohead, along with Oasis and REM, [are] were his ideal headliners for the first Glastonbury of the new millennium.

As the year drew to a close there was a brief flurry of [Radiohead] activity. On November 24th their film *Meeting People Is Easy* premiered at the Metro cinema in London's West End, just under a week before it hit the shops. It was the result of fly-on-the-wall footage that Grant Gee, the director of the promo for 'No Surprises', had been taking of the band since the Barcelona dates at the start of the *Ok Computer* tour. Gee described the film as "a bunch of articulate, essentially shy people who . . . find themselves in the strange/insane/seductive world of end-of the-century celebrity, with thousands of cameras and microphones constantly siphoning little bits off them". The film is in keeping with Radiohead's distinctive imagery, as the band, chatting backstage in Barcelona, are viewed as an information over-load of text and newsprint scrolls down the screen. Indeed *Meeting People Is Easy* depicted a band weary of the rigours of touring and the relentless publicity machine surrounding them.

Radiohead's commitment to playing for political causes continued in December when they headlined the Amnesty International 50th anniversary concert at the Bercy Stadium in Paris. Although they played no new material the gig, in front of the 16,000 crowd was generally seen as a triumph.

Then, in a strange end to the year, a group calling themselves the SPU.N.K.L.E. Allstars released a single on Oxford based label Shifty Disco that sampled a Radiohead gig from 1992. However, the band didn't seem to mind, as a spokeswoman put it "We get calls everyday about people doing Radiohead stuff in one way or another. Honestly, they're not really bothered."

Such indifference can be seen as a reflection of more serious internal problems within the band at this time. For it was becoming clear that public adulation had taken a personal toll. After so long on the commercial treadmill, the group was running on empty. And other artists sampling their work was a minor problem compared to what lay ahead . . .

**'When some guy comes up
and buys you a drink and says that**

**the last record you made changed
his life, it means something.'**

< CHAPTER: 10 >

EVERYTHING ALL THE TIME

"I tell you what's really ridiculous – going into a bookshop and there's all these books about yourself. In a way it feels like you're already dead. So you've got a kind of license to start again." **Thom**

The truth was that by the end of 1998, Radiohead were burnt out after a momentous period comprising a hectic schedule of live dates and promotional activities. But for Thom, problems ran deeper. And they surfaced when he was faced with the prospect of recording the follow-up to *OK Computer*.

Thom wrestled with deeply ambivalent feelings about the direction of the group as a whole, and his role within in it. These manifested in considerations about how to progress as a band and as a human being with any integrity, in the face of the massive success that subsumed Radiohead into the world of commerce. Contemplation of such issues was hardly new territory for Thom, and is of course an inherent part of Radiohead, but Thom had moved beyond his enduring existential angst to a point where these issues became all encompassing. He withdrew completely. It was not until several years later that Thom gave his public an insight into this enormously painful time in his life. In a magazine interview in late 2000 he stated, "I was a complete fucking mess! When *OK Computer* finished I was really, really ill. Just going a certain way for a long, long time and not being able to stop of look back or consider where I was. For, like, ten years. Not being able to connect with anything. Becoming completely unhinged, in the best sense of the word.' In another interview he went on to say, 'I always used to use music as a way of moving on and dealing with things and I sort of felt like, that the thing that helped me deal with things had been sold to the highest bidder and I was simply doing its bidding' These feelings were never stronger than on New Year's Eve 1998, which Thom told Q was "one of the lowest points in my life. I felt like I was going fucking crazy. Every time I picked up a guitar I just got the horrors. I would start writing a song, stop after 16 bars, hide it away in a drawer, look at it again, tear it up, destroy it . . . I was sinking down and down."

Thom and the rest of Radiohead were to find creative salvation in the making of their fourth album, but initial recording sessions proved tortuous. In January 1999, they convened in the Studio Guillaume in Paris. Besides the fact that Thom, suffering from writer's block, had barely any new material to present to the rest of the group, inter-band dynamics were fraught and uneasy. They ran through tracks they'd been working on for the past year, such as 'Lost At Sea', but it soon became apparent that the tried and tested method of gathering in a room to rehearse and jam, was no longer working. What also emerged was that band members had very different ideas about the direction the new album should take. Ed still favoured a traditionalist approach, and believed it would be refreshing to adhere to the classic rock blueprint with an album of three-minute songs. But for Thom this was anathema. Such discussion only served to propel him further into crisis. As he told Q, "Fucking hell, there was no chance of the album sounding like that, I'd completely had it with melody. I just wanted rhythm. All melodies to me were pure embarassment"

By March the band had endured similarly difficult sessions in Copenhagen's Medley Studios, producing little in the way of new material and continuing their nomadic existence into April, when they set up camp in the secluded Gloucestershire mansion Barsford Park. They hardly needed it, but there was a practical impediment adding to Radiohead's problems – they were not going to be able to enter their own recording studio until September 1999, as its refurbishment was taking longer than expected. It was at Barsford Park that Radiohead were forced to confront themselves. The making of the album had become a make or break situation for the group. Both as friends and band-mates they felt tired and jaded, the situation further compounded by creative differences. Wholly dismayed by the difficulties of resolving these personal issues and deciding on their new direction, Radiohead were on the verge of splitting up.

One major problem was that the rest of the band had a hard time grasping the concepts and methodologies that Thom envisaged for the new album. He wanted to make the leap from guitar and vocal led musical constructions to wider ranging experiments in sound. For a band comprising no less than four guitarists, used to working around highly distinctive vocals, this was hard to bear. But Thom was adamant that in terms of personal and artistic growth, assimilating a greater range of influences into Radiohead's sound was the right thing to do.

Much has been made of Thom's admiration for the artists on the pioneering techno label Warp, cited as a huge influence on the album. And Thom has made no secret of the fact that the work of those such as Aphex Twin and Autechre provided him with a starting point: as he told Q, 'The first thing I did after the [*OK Computer*] tour was buy the whole Warp back catalogue. I started listening to John Peel and ordering records off the Net. It was refreshing because the music was all structures and had no human voices on it. But I felt just as emotional about it as I'd ever felt about guitar music.' Of course Thom's interest in electronic music stretches back to his college days, when he flirted with the rave scene, being blown away by records like Sweet Exorcist's 'Per Clonk' at parties, joining the techno outfit Flickernoise, and experimenting with music-making via sequencers. OK Computer had already showed that Radiohead were capable of building electronic noise into rock constructs with stunning results and a series of respected dance artists performed remix duties on Radiohead tracks in subsequent years. LFO remixed 'Planet Telex', while Zero 7 and Fila Brazilia delivered re-workings of 'Climbing The Walls'.

'If you're going to make a different sounding record, you have to change the methodology. And it's scary – everyone feels insecure.'

Despite this, the idea of making such electronic noise the all-pervasive element in their next recording proved to be a big step. This was a creative leap, and a commercial risk that no one in Radiohead took lightly. Ed later explained 'If you're going to make a different sounding record, you have to change the methodology. And it's scary – everyone feels insecure. I'm a guitarist and suddenly it's like, well, there are no guitars on this track, or no drums. Jonny, me, Coz, and Phil had to get our heads around that. It was a test of the band, I think. Would we survive with our egos intact?'

Plagued by such questions, in the summer of 1999, Ed began an online diary on the Radiohead website which proved to be compulsive reading for fans and press, yet initially revealed no more than confusion. 'The problem is that we are essentially in limbo. For the first time we have nothing to get ready for, except 'an album', but we've been working on that since January and nothing substantial has come of it, except maybe a few harsh lessons in how not to do things . . .'

It seemed Parlophone's decision to give the band as long as they needed to produce a new album had created nothing more than a vacuum. The band moved into their own studio by September 1999, and continued grappling with new ideas, accommodating themselves to working on sounds rather than songs. But it was not until January 1999 that Radiohead really began to understand how, in Ed's words, 'to be a participant in a song without playing a note.'

Radiohead's producer, Nigel Godrich played a pivotal role. He took Thom's ideas and ran with them, encouraging the group to experiment and improvise with recording techniques and ways of working. The band was inspired, and took the final turn from destruction into construction. Jonny, ever the multi-instrumentalist, re-discovered his passion for the Ondes Martenot, a curious instrument which is most famous for the wailing sound of the Star Wars theme. Ed finally came alive to the possibilites of synthesisers, and Thom revelled in distorting his voice to the degree where it became just another sound array of instrumentation, through everything from state of the art studio equipment to pieces of cardboard. The influence of a whole host of progressive artists and producers also came into play. Radiohead drew inspiration from Holger Czukay's innovative production work for legendary group Can, Brian Eno's work on the Radiohead favourite *Remain in Light* by Talking Heads, and Michael Stipe's work on the REM album *Monster*. A special album for Thom was *The Complete Town Hall Concert* by legendary jazz bassist Charlie Mingus.

'You're lying if you're pretending it's not a product, that you're not trying to sell something.'

Creative collaborations that took place around this time showed just how far Radiohead had moved on from gloomy introspection to dynamic enthusiasm. In early 2000, Thom collaborated with Bjork on the soundtrack to her film, *Dancer in the Dark*. There had always been a great deal of mutual admiration between the two artists, and Bjork had nothing but praise for Thom's efforts. She went on record as saying 'I thought that I finally had a song that deserved his voice, 'cause he's my favourite male singer in the world. I asked him, and he being the kind of guy he is, full of integrity; there's not a grain of artificial show-business behaviour in him – he kind of insisted he would turn up and be there for quite a while, so the communication in the song, the recording, was real and genuine.' Meanwhile Jonny left the Orchestra of St John starry eyed, when he employed the services of the world renowned Oxford ensemble on four album tracks.

The intense period of activity had produced a wealth of material. By April 2000 the band had recorded some sixty tracks, and selected ten for the album: 'Everything In It's Right Place', 'Kid A', 'The National Anthem', 'How To Disappear Completely', 'Treefingers', 'Optimistic', 'In Limbo', 'Idioteque', 'Morning Bell' and 'Motion Picture Soundtrack'. The album itself was entitled *Kid A*. Inevitably, there was great speculation about the album's name. Some claimed that it was taken from a computer program containing children's voices, while others suggested that it was derived from the character of the same name in Carl Steadman's book *Alphabet Street*. However, Thom offered another explanation on the band's official message board. *Kid A* was 'dedicated to the first human clone. I bet it has already happened.' A similar chill of ambiguity surrounded the album as a whole. The radical approach that had galvanised production was now being applied to promotion. While Radiohead had given out some information about *Kid A* via their website, (though Ed had stopped his diary due to the press generating news stories from it) it was a different story with the more conventional forms of media. There were to be no singles released from the album, which meant no radio airplay, and no videos accompanying the music, which meant no exposure on MTV. Press interviews were to be conducted by email, and the band declined to engage in all but the bare minimum of any other promotional activity.

What was crystal clear from this plan of non-action, was that Radiohead wished to operate on their own terms. They had learnt a bitter lesson in the wake of *OK Computer* and were determined at all costs to avoid the physical exhaustion and emotional stultification they had experienced. Also key to the way they approached *Kid A* was their ever increasing levels of politicisation. They had always been a band with a social conscience, but being trapped inside the commercial machine after *OK Computer* had reinforced their ideals. They wholeheartedly supported the global anti-capitalist movement, which gained momentum in 2000 with the publication of *No Logo* by Naomi Klein, a book which laid bare capitalist practices and principles. Ed enthusiastically recommended the book to fans in his online diary, and later said told *Q*, '*No Logo* gave one real hope. It certainly made me feel less alone. I must admit I'm deeply pessimistic about humanity, and she was writing everything that I was trying to make sense of in my head. It was very uplifting.' Spurred on, during 2000, Ed participated in the in the Anti-World Trade Organisation march in Whitehall, while Thom had been involved in the Jubilee 2000 campaign against third world debt since 1999, when he, along with U2's Bono had attempted to deliver a petition in to the G8 summit in Cologne.

However, this did not mean, as some press reports implied, that Radiohead had ceased to communicate with the outside world. In fact they found inventive ways of getting their message across. They planned a 'Tent Tour' for later in the year, deciding to run concerts from a 10,000 capacity tent that would be a logo free environment banning brand names or advertising. Meanwhile, select journalists were presented with copies of the album stored electronically in Sony VAOI Music Clips. (Storing the album on these pocket-size digital players was also a move against piracy, but the album found its way onto Napster anyway). And for public consumption, the band arranged to broadcast the whole album, complete with animation on MTV 2. They would also screen a series of 10 to 40 second animated video 'blips', first on the Internet, containing soundbites from the album, first on select Radiohead sites and then on MTV's main channel. Thom described the thinking behind this move in interviews: 'The thing that really did my head in was going home and turning on the TV and the ads for fucking banks and cars being more like MTV videos than the MTV videos, and it seemed like there was nowhere to go. Whatever the new aesthetic was would be in a fucking car advert a week later. Especially Colin, he got obsessed over not making videos and making adverts. Because the ads were more like the videos, so we might as well go straight to the source. You're lying if you're pretending it's not a product, that you're not trying to sell something. It wasn't like we sat down and said, 'How do we do things differently?' Neccessity meant that we had to.'

This 'blip' animation meanwhile, was echoed in the artwork for *Kid A*. Spreading across the album cover and continuing into a multi-page, multi-layered booklet, it comprised images of a glacial and ravaged landscape peopled by tiny beings, plus a more distinct image of Tony Blair. Combining collage, computer graphics and simple sketch lines in black, blue and white hues, the whole effect was eerie yet moving, suggesting the familiar Radiohead themes of alienation and vulnerability. Something completely unfamilar to fans, however was a lack of written lyrics in the album inlay. As part of his move away from vocal led music, Thom had not even explained the album's sparse lyrics to his band-mates. Many were random words and phrases quite literally pulled out of a (top) hat filled with scrawls on scraps that he kept in the studio throughout recording sessions.

Although, this abtruse approach was confusing for Radiohead's audience, it did mean that the band's return to the live stage was greeted with extra fervour. In June 2000, they hit the road to preview *Kid A* and roadtest the new material before the autumn's Tent Tour. They made their first appearance since 1998 onstage in Barcelona, before a crowd of fanatical fans who had already downloaded the album from the Internet, and an assortment of curious music journalists. Belting out classics such as 'Karma Police' alongside the new material, the gig was the final confirmation that Radiohead had regained confidence and were – shock horror – having fun! Thom's pleasure was evident when he addressed the crowd at the end of the gig with a huge smile, and said, 'Thank you for being so nice on our first gig back.'

As the band played a series of low key dates around Europe they found that their new material, in particular the tracks 'How To Disappear Completely And Never Be Found', and 'Everything In Its Right Place', made a deep emotional impact on audiences. The band's return to the UK was similarly triumphant. In July they played the Meltdown Festival at the personal request of Scott Walker, delivering an unforgettable performance, integrating sampling effects into Thom's vocals, and being relaxed enough to laugh it off when 'My Iron Lung' fell apart halfway through. Thom said afterwards, 'We did that gig for him basically. I was on stage thinking Scott Walker's in the audience.'

Someone else Thom has much admiration for is PJ Harvey, and around this time her seventh album, 'Stories From The City, Stories From The Sea', was released, featuring a duet with Thom called 'This Mess We're In', plus two other tracks he sings on called 'Beautiful Feeling' and 'One Line'. This release was also very well received and demonstrated that Radiohead maintained not just the respect of fans but also many of their peers.

'Once we finished this record I started being easier on myself because I understood a little better where I was supposed to be.'

The band left the UK for more dates in Europe, then returned to play a similarly intense gig at Victoria Park in late September. After they had presented an awesome rendition of 'The National Anthem', Thom simply stated, 'There's been enough bullshit said already so we're not going to say anything tonight, ' and the band delivered a powerful set in which past classics like 'My Iron Lung' sat easily with the *Kid A* material.

But although Radiohead had captivated their hardcore following with these performances, they still had mainstream opinion to deal with. They were after all a world famous rock band, which had gone out on a limb with an album of electronic beats and bleeps. This had been a fantastic challenge for them, but would be an unexpected challenge for the wider audience. When *Kid A* was released in October 2000, the initial reaction was one of shock and derision. Press reviews were often venomous, and the best that can be said of them is that they had some comic value.

Melody Maker described the album as an 'avalanche of electronic mice, pointless vocoder twattery and baboon rape', going on to argue that 'They've created a monument of effect over content, a smothery cataclysm of sound and fury signifying precisely f*** all.' Q magazine could muster nothing more than indifference, declaiming the album as 'as about as experimental as a major rock record could get within the corporate straight-jacket that Radiohead despise,' and once again drawing comparisons with Pink Floyd. In America the response was similarly negative: although fans sent *Kid A* to number one, even Rolling Stone denounced it as being difficult to listen to.

Kid A initially caused a furore, but over time the album came to be regarded as a remarkable excursion into electronic realms, which broadened the concept of post-rock. And, as the driving force behind the album, Thom, throughout, wears not only his heart, but also his influences on his sleeve. Even if Radiohead had released singles for *Kid A*, it would have been clear from listening to it that it is intended to be experienced as a whole. The album opens with 'Everything In Its Right Place', which combines organ notes and Thom's cut up vocals to form a stark electronic soundscape, floating in deep-sea beats. The fragmented vocals and increasingly insistent chords crescendo throughout, and as Thom's voice becomes increasingly fraught, these effects combine to create the song's emotional power. It's no wonder that 'Everything In Its Right Place' received such a positive reception when it was first heard live on the tent-tour.

The album's title track, 'Kid A', opens with soft ambient chimes. Thom's voice, distorted through a vocoder, transforms it into a robotic lullaby, then gives way to spiky beats. Punctuated throughout by scattered electronic chitterings, like the gurglings of a synthetic baby, 'Kid A' reminds us of the laboratory origins of its imaginary namesake.

In contrast, 'The National Anthem' juxtaposes a fuzzy, funky base guitar and rock drums with electronic embellishments. It seems to cover more familiar ground until it breaks into a Charlie Mingus inspired frenzy of sax and horns. Thom's vocals remain distorted and are supported by a recurrent theramin-like wailing, which questions the unbridled enthusiasm of the jazz instrumentation. The presence of the eight-man brass band, as used by Mingus in his album, highlights the distortion of Thom's voice, which becomes one amongst a host of synthesised effects. The track is held together throughout by the stabilising presence of the bass guitar which, like the vocals, is a halfway house between the acoustic sounds of the brass instruments and the pure electronica of the effects.

This counterpoint of the acoustic and the electronic prepares the way for the song which proved to be the critics favourite. If 'The National Anthem' had a familiar flavour, 'How To Disappear Completely And Never Be Found' is *Kid A*'s nearest offering to vintage Radiohead. Ironically, it is on this track that Thom's voice is furthest from disappearing. With a title drawn from an American self help book, this opus had been generating speculation even before Radiohead entered the studio in 1999, and with good reason. It promised to be the most intense song on the album. The band had premiered initial versions of 'How To Disappear Completely . . .' on their last US tour, when it had been hailed as music with epic qualities, and this was borne out by reactions to Thom's heart-rending renditions of it during gigs in 2000. For the final version Jonny spent two weeks on his own scoring strings, putting his past music studies to good use.

On 'Treefingers' Thom's vocals actually do disappear in a track heavily indebted to Aphex Twin. Of all the tracks on the album, it is this which best demonstrates the band's modest ethos, as expressed by Jonny – "We don't sit down and say, 'Let's break barriers'. We just copy our favourite records." 'Treefingers' comes as close as Radiohead ever could to pure ambience, but despite being the album's greatest departure from Radiohead's previous style, it still acknowledges their musical foundations: resting on what seem to be synthesisers, the song is actually based on an elongated guitar sample.

The next track, 'Optimistic', again relies heavily on guitar sounds, contradicting the "what no guitar?" complaints of some disgruntled critics and fans. Thom's vocals conjure an image of a wasteland of exploitation and compromise, where even the pigs led to the slaughter pack a payload. 'Optimistic' is a jaded fairytale of lost innocence. At it's close it relaxes into comfortable jazz only to see 'In Limbo' picking up where 'Optimistic' leaves off, turning the harmonious end on its head with the accusation, 'You're living in a fantasy world'. It sucks us down into a sonic representation of an emotional whirlpool.

'Idioteque' immerses the listener into an arch evocation of yet another fantasy world. It's crunching two step beats take us onto the dance floor. Described by *Q* as 'about as uplifting as Mandrax' but by *NME* as 'the album's saving grace,' for fans 'Idioteque' is a track more loved than hated. It uses the contemporary sounds of dance to criticise comtemporary evils. It tells a tale of a society rife with excess – 'Everything all the time,' is its repeated refrain.

With 'Morning Bell', Radiohead unashamedly display their musical dexterity, taking in punchy live drumming and Rhode's piano arrangements built around Thom's aching vocals. It's evocation of divorce conjures impressions both of freedom and suffering, mirrored by the contrast between the harrowing voice and soothing piano duet. One line of 'Morning Bell' was inspired by the letter Thom received, saying it was a shame that Jeff Buckley had died and not him.

The final listed track, 'Motion Picture Soundtrack' was written at the same time as *OK Computer* and first heard on the album tour. It has been compared to 'Exit Music (For A Film)', and certainly shares that song's ambivalent beauty . Introduced by a church organ, Thom's subdued vocals root us in the mud of life before a flurry of harps floats us up towards the song's close. A 1950s movie style angelic choir accompanies the closing line, "I will see you in the next life", which overturns the song's initial atmosphere of loss and depression. We are left with a sense of reconcilliation, and the song becomes a funeral celebration. It's poignancy comes from the suggestion, evoked by the movie-soundtrack references, that heaven may merely be a comfortable fiction. 'Motion Picture Soundtrack', *Kid A*'s closing intimation of hope and insecurity cohabiting, is finally punctuated by the album's hidden track – a ten second blast of white noise.

The process of recording *Kid A* and presenting it to the rest of the world had provided Radiohead with some kind of emotional catharsis. Live, they were stronger than ever, as performances throughout their autumn 'Tent Tour' proved. At number one in the American album charts, they also made an appearance on NBC's Saturday Night Live, and enjoyed performing stunning versions of 'Idioteque' and 'The National Anthem'. Their relationship with the press had also improved, though it was still ambivalent: for September 2000 they agreed to a feature in *Q*, yet doctored images of themselves by cutting out their eyes. But the following month they launched 'Spin With A Grin', an area of the Radiohead website intended to aid journalists.

Meanwhile the band's relationship with fans remained completely solid. In December Thom, Jonny and Colin thrilled their audience with a a live DJ set on BBC Radio 1. They had aired similar sets from their website since 1999, but a BBC broadcast suggested a band that was comfortable with their status and impact. As Thom stated in a later interview, 'Once we finished this record I started being easier on myself, because I understood a little bit better where I was supposed to be. All the way through making *Kid A* I was faced with the prospect of thinking, "Maybe it'll never happen." I managed to get sounds out of my head and onto tape as much as we could, and that meant I could be a little bit happier about the place I was at.' In the private domain there was also a great deal of happiness for Thom, as at the end of the year he became a father to baby Noah with long-time girlfriend Rachel.

There was more triumph to come in 2001 when *Kid A* began to receive the recognition it deserved. In February Phil, Colin and Ed found themselves at the Grammys in the US, collecting the award for Best Alternative Rock album. Thom and Jonny, who had managed to wriggle out of attending, watched it all from the comfort of their sofas.

Jonny was amused: 'the three of them looked so awkward the audience all started laughing.' Colin confirmed this when he said, 'It felt like any minute we'd be ejected by the organisers screaming, "What are you doing in the same room as all these Playboy bunnies?". Ed however dealt with it in his own way: "I actually took some mushrooms that night. It was the best thing to do; going round the parties afterwards – there were fires everywhere and swimming pools and 'the beautiful people' – it was like being on a film set."

Radiohead were also given recognition by the British industry when they were nominated for Best Group and Best album at the Brit awards in February. Although both awards went to Coldplay, fans fiercely contested the decision. But in the same month readers of NME voted Radiohead Best Group Ever, which indicated that whatever the whims of the industry, the strength and loyalty of their fanbase remained undiminished.

Radiohead's fans were now eagerly awaiting the arrival of their fifth album, entitled *Amnesiac*. Online chat rooms and message boards buzzed with speculation and news about the forthcoming release, and Thom often joined discussions on the official

'Originally it was about the voices in my head that were driving me around the bend – to be honest.'

Radiohead site. As well as giving news on the album's content, his comments indicated that Radiohead, having made their point with minimal publicity for *Kid A*, would be taking a more relaxed approach with the new album. At one point Thom stated that the band 'are really proud of *Amnesiac* and we want to give it a fair chance within the giant scary cogs of the bullshit machine.' He also caused surprise when he joked that the release of the album would come complete with 'singles, videos, glossy magazine celebrity photo-shoots, children's television appearances, film premiere appearances, dance routines, and many interesting interviews about my tortured existence'.

But while Radiohead were cheerfully resigned to their promotional duties, musically they were determined to continue forging their own path. Thom made this clear when he told one fansite, 'It's really exciting to go back into the studio now feeling confident again, having learnt different stuff . . . having to learn to play music that was written in the studio using editing, sampling and sequencers . . . the way it makes you think about how you play differently . . . perhaps nowadays we look more to Can and electronica to work out how to structure stuff'. With these considerations in mind, the band had assembled Amnesiac from material recorded during *Kid A*, plus some new compositions. Their main aim was to keep experimenting, progressing, and staying outside convention. As Colin said, they were 'keeping it going, y, know, not be like a boring rock band and do an album every two years.' Meanwhile Thom gave a typically creative description of what Amnesiac would sound like compared to *Kid A*, saying that the first album, 'well, that's the fire from afar', while the new album, 'would be like standing in the fire.'

Any comparisons between *Kid A* and *Amnesiac* were inevitable, given that much of *Amnesiac* was recorded at the same time as *Kid A*, and that both albums had a predominantly electronic sound, combined with deeply personalised content from Thom. However, when *Amnesiac* was released in June 2001, it was clear that the album was no *Kid A* spin off. As Thom explained, 'It was all finished around the same time as *Kid A*. That's why it was quite hard. We had like a board of sketches, a list of about 60 sketches – some of which were songs, others just sequences or ideas for sounds. Then it got narrowed down and narrowed down until we had a block of stuff which felt like it fitted together. And then *Kid A* pulled itself together very easily and very obviously. But Amnesiac didn't.'

But eventually *Amnesiac* did take on a life of its own, and each track tells its own story. Whittled down from around 24 tracks, the final track listing was 'Packt Like Sardines In A Crushed Tin Box' 'Pyramid Song', 'Pulk/Pull Revolving Doors', 'You and Whose Army?', 'I Might Be Wrong', 'Knives Out', 'Amnesiac/Morning Bell', 'Dollars and Cents', 'Hunting Bears', 'Like Spinning Plates', and 'Life In A Glass House'. 'Pyramid Song' had already been chosen for release as a single in May, when it went to number 5 in the charts, and was widely, and rightly, regarded as one of the album's strongest tracks. Recorded in the same week as 'Everything In It's Right Place', and inspired by a Thom's obsession with the Charlie Mingus song, 'Freedom', the track is underpinned by Thom playing black keys on a piano. Murmuring strings fade in and out of hearing until they crescendo into a swirling current in which Thom's floating vocals eddy and turn . What really gratified fans however, was the song's accessibility; Thom's ethereal vocals are clearer than on *Kid A*, buoyed up, rather than drowned, by gentle drums and instrumentation.

Fans fell in love with other tracks on the album for similar reasons. 'Knives Out' and 'You and Whose Army' had already been huge crowd pleasers at gigs the previous year, as they were both more straightforward guitar-based songs. Fans had been speculating since then as to whether they would appear on *Amnesiac*. 'Knives Out', builds indie guitars around Thom's vocals, called 'a collage of playground taunts' by Q. The lyrics do have the tone of school-boy teasing, but only if we're listening to bullies in some twisted cannibal nursery. The haunting guitars and surreal, disjointed lyrics remind us more of remembered taunts, returning like ghosts. Throughout the song the guitars have a strange lyricism, as if despite the pain which the memories evoke, they are also accompanied by nostalgia. In a typical knee-jerk rejection, Thom disowned his progeny: 'for the longest time I really, really hated that song'. But reaction to 'Knives Out' had been so positive, that it was eventually released as a single in August, when just as 'Pyramid Song' had done, it went to number 5 in the charts.

'You and Whose Army?' stirred up interest, as much for its politics as its sound. Thom told *Mojo*, 'Originally it was about the voices in my head that were driving me round the bend – to be honest. And then, once I came up with that 'You And Whose Army' phrase, I was able to stick other ideas on there and Blair emerged as the song's real subject matter. The song's ultimately about someone who is elected into power by people and who then blatantly betrays them, just like Blair did.' Surprisingly, given the subject matter, 'You and Whose Army?' is not an angry song. Although it pays lip service to the aggression which dogs political protest, 'Come on if you think you can take us on' repeats Yorke, the music and singing themselves are shot through with weariness. These demonstrators would lie down in front of tanks rather than throw petrol bombs. Inspired by the harmonising of 1940s group the Ink Spots, The song's haunting impact was enhanced when Radiohead filtered all the instruments and vocals through an egg box.

'I Might Be Wrong' meanwhile, is another guitar led track that showed how the strong the group are as a unit; as comfortable with instumental music as they are layering electronic sounds and textures. Created with a drum machine specially built by Jonny and a great bass-line delivered by Colin who 'had it in mind that I was Bernard Edwards that night', it went on to become the first US single from the album.

'Hunting Bears', entirely comprised of guitar and effects, was a similarly spartan but no less powerful track. The title also elicited curiosity, given the band's 'blinkybear' logo. Thom has since explained the bear metaphor: 'it stemmed intially from a deep paranoia of genetic engineering. And then from a children's book. You know, creating monsters only to awake one morning to the terrible truth there is nothing you can do to stop them. We're over it now.'

Throughout Amnesiac, however, the influence of electronic music is still strong. With it's techno feel, the opening track, 'Packt Like Sardines' drew comparisons with Underworld, Autechre and Aphex Twin, although Ed felt that it was one of the most upbeat tracks on the album! The track opens with spare syncopated beats before the slowly pulsing bass introduces Thom's distorted vocals. Yorke's voice was filtered through an Autotuner, a machine used to produce robotic sounding vocals. However Radiohead pre-programmed it to reveal technological idiosyncrasies, and in doing so created a unique sound. The Autotuner was also used on Pull/Pulk Revolving Doors, where Thom's stream of consciousness style vocals are set against jagged dance beats. 'Dollars and Cents', another track which had caused a stir when performed live, continues this experimental theme, piecing together musical fragments into sweeping strings that work up to electronic jazz.

In a similar vein, 'Like Spinning Plates', another piece of glittering electronica, was built from a song called 'I Will', played backwards. This was the kind of experimentation Thom loved: 'We'd turned the tape around, and I was in another room, heard the vocal melody coming backwards, and thought, 'That's miles better than the right way round, then spent the rest of the night trying to learn the melody'. Opening with choppy syncopated sounds, the song mutates into a nightmare merrygoround tune. 'Like Spinning Plates', became Thom's favourite track on the album: 'In terms of trying to get somewhere new, I think 'Spinning Plates' is the best of all the records for me. When I listen to it in my car, it makes the doors shake.'

'Amnesiac/Morning Bell' forms the album's electronic centrepiece. It is an emotive version of *Kid A*'s ambivalent evocation of divorce which displays Radiohead's mastery in combining seemingly disparate musical elements. Yet it is darker in tone. Where *Kid A*'s version disolves into ambiguity, with lines such as 'Cut the kids in half', 'Amnesiac/Morning Bell' describes the harsh realities of divorce with razor-sharp clarity.

The album ends with 'Life In A Glass House', a 'New Orleans funeral march' to mourn lost friendship, according to *Q*, and for which Radiohead procured the services of revered jazz trumpeter Humphrey Littleton. The song is perhaps the album's best demonstration of Yorke's highly metaphorical lyrical style, constantly implying ideas rather than stating them. What results is a stately evocation of guilt and loss, tinged with an inability entirely to assign or accept blame.

The album's artwork was also in keeping with the whole tone of the piece. To Radiohead, the appearance was of paramount importance. As Thom said, 'For me it's an integral part of the record itself. I know this sounds wanky but it's true: if the music's not inspiring the pictures then I'm not comfortable. *Amnesiac* is packaged like a closed book.' The album, quite literally, was encased as a hardback library book, that even had an authentically stamped slip. Inside was a 28 page colour booklet which contained detailed colour plate illustrations created by Thom and Stanley Donwood.

Overall, the presentation of the album served to emphasise Radiohead's more communicative mood. This certainly had an effect, as *Amnesiac* was generally well received by the press. Naturally, after *Kid A*, the album came as less of a shock, but it was also acclaimed as an impressive piece of work in its own right. Q magazine delivered the final verdict with the sentence, '*Amnesiac* is similarly shy, textural and embroidered by electronica, but where it differs vitally from *Kid A* is in being 1) better balanced, 2) more emotionally intelligible and 3) even more grimly beautiful.' Across the water, the US press were also far more receptive, *Blender* magazine describing the album as, 'a lovely emotive and tune-challenged collision between futuristic electronics, old fashioned orchestration and the band's tender songwriting.' *Amnesiac* was then nominated for the Mercury Music Prize given in July, although the award went to PJ Harvey's album, *Stories From The City, Stories From The Sea*. The fact that Thom's vocals featured on three tracks appeased Radiohead fans somewhat! The fans themselves loved *Amnesiac*, which debuted at number one worldwide.

In conjunction with the album release, Radiohead embarked on a world tour, their first since 1997. Expectations and emotions among fans ran high, but this time Radiohead were full of enthusiasm, and after an enjoyable round of rehearsals, were ready to rock. Said Thom in one pre-tour interview, 'It's great. The songs are coming easily. It's just really nice. We've all got our confidence back.' And Johnny was pleased too: 'It's all loud and it's all guitars. It's exciting to make loud music again. It's sounding new and fresh.'

Radiohead toured Europe and the US in June, came back to the UK for July and returned to the US in August, closing with shows in Japan in October. For the fans who attended shows, Radiohead delivered everything they wished for, with a series of electrifying performances that also won plaudits from the world's press. And their performance on home-ground, headlining the South Park Festival in Oxford on July 7th, went down in history as one of their best ever. Despite an ominously grey sky, 40,000 people attended to witness Radiohead, supported by Humphrey Littleton, Signor Ros, Supergrass and Beck. Driving the crowd into a frenzy with cuts from *Kid A* and *Amnesiac*, including heartfelt renditions of 'Pyramid Song' and 'How to Disappear Completely', the band then launched into old classics. 'My Iron Lung' provoked such a serious crush as the crowd surged forward, that security had to step in, but there were also lighter moments, as when Thom dedicated 'Paranoid Android' to Geri Halliwell! In an emotional finale the band played no less than three encores, at which point the heavens opened and Thom's synth also failed. However the band played on, and astonishingly, ended their set with 'Creep', a huge surprise, which was pure magic for fans.

Always a band with a social conscience, Radiohead donated much of the profits from the South Park show to worthy causes in their home-town, including hospitals, shelter units, and their old friends the Orchestra of St John's, who received £20,000. It was a touching end to an emotional round of touring which had seen Radiohead re-establish their relationship with fans all over the world. In October, readers of *Q* magazine voted Radiohead Best Band In The World for the magazine's annual awards ceremony, and fans were subsequently thrilled with the release of Radiohead's first live album in November. Entitled *I Might Be Wrong – Live Recordings*, the album contained live versions of *Kid A* and *Amnesiac* tracks, plus the title track 'I Might Be Wrong', which had become a staple of their live sets.

'It's all loud and it's all guitars. It's exciting to make loud music again. It's sounding new and fresh.'

After the world tour, Radiohead gave themselves six months off. This was something the band felt they had to do. In a later interview in NME, Thom said, 'it was the longest we've ever had off. We were sending tapes to each other with ideas. Which is how we did *OK Computer*'. This statement was indicative of the fact that Thom's creative methods were becoming much more straightforward. In a departure from his approach to *Kid A* and *Amnesiac* he now allowed the band to see lyrics and build songs around them, which was an approach they had always felt very comfortable with.

Thom's creative journey, finding suitable ways of thinking and working, was also changing how he felt at a personal level. Interviews given in 2001 revealed someone who had learned to live with their personal demons. Speaking to NME on the subject of his perceived depression, he declared, 'It's not particulary destructive, it's not particularly bad. Lots of people are much worse – lots of people can't leave the house. They've got no idea why, maybe they will never find out why. The drugs they get given don't work, and all the therapy is completely pointless. A lot of creative people hear voices, a lot of creative people have crazy thoughts, a lot of creative people want to jump off bridges. So fucking what . . . ?'

For Thom, the answer to that question centres on the fact that he is part of Radiohead, and has to deal with the all the responsibilities and expectations that his position brings. 2002 was no different. In the new year, while they were busy writing new material, Radiohead were once again thrust into the limelight when they were nominated for a series of awards. *Kid A* was nominated for Best British album at the

Brit awards, and the band were nominated for Best Group. They didn't win these, but in February Ed and Colin attended the collect the Best Video prize at the *NME* Carling awards for 'Pyramid Song'. In true Radiohead style they did not bask in glory, and when cornered by an *NME* journalist, gave typically understated responses to questions, with Ed stating that 'we didn't actually have anything to do with the video at all. So it's vaguely embarassing to be here for this, because it's not ours.' February also saw the band venerated in the US as they were also nominated for Best Band, Best Album and Best Live Act at the Grammys. Thom attended the awards ceremony this time, and although again the band did not win in any of the categories, the hat trick of nominations cemented their status.

'A lot of creative people hear voices, a lot of creative people have crazy thoughts, a lot of creative people want to jump off bridges. So fucking what?'

However, Radiohead had never been the kind of band to care about industry recognition and continued to be more involved in making and playing music than anything else. While Thom was in America he played with Beck at a charity gig in LA for the Recording Artists Coaltion, before joining the rest of his band-mates to begin recording the follow-up to *Amnesiac* in March. Rumours about Radiohead's next move were rife, so fans were disappointed to learn that there would be no UK gigs, including no Glastonbury appearance in 2002. But Radiohead were determined that recording the new album had to be their priority.

Such prioritising was highly necessary. Once again, recording was going to be an all-consuming process, as Radiohead had no fixed plans for the new album's sound. In NME, March 2002, Ed would only offer the following words, 'We don't know what it will sound like yet. You get asked this question before you make a record and we just don't know. So many times you say it's going to be the three minute pop record, and other times you say it's the prog rock record and it never turns out that way. We'll just get back into the rehearsal studio and we'll see what happens'. In fact, the band, now older, wiser and stronger, spent April and May rehearsing new songs, and completed a short tour of Spain and Portugal in the summer to test out crowd reaction, before they even set foot in the studio that autumn.

The short European tour went fantastically well, and once again confirmed Radiohead as a truly international band, with a hugely committed fanbase. Fans recorded the live shows and posted them onto Internet fansites for download, fuelling speculation as to which tracks would eventually be included on the album. Tracks generating the greatest interest included 'There There', 'Myxomatosis' and 'Sail To The Moon'.

Radiohead themselves really enjoyed the tour, with Colin naming it, 'the Creative Gentleman's Leisurely Tour,' taking in venues hand-picked by Ed, and playing out around sixteen new songs to ecstatic crowds, who relished the band's return to a guitar infused sound. One highlight was their performance at the Benicassim festival in Barcelona, where the band delivered a startlingly intense performance. But onstage and offstage Thom's cheerful mood was evident, as he frequently made physical contact with audiences, pulling faces, shaking hands and even dancing with them. He also joked with interviewers about the heavy, grinding style of the new material with interviewers: 'some of the rhythms are definitely for shagging. If you like to shag very, very slowly. At 80bpm.' Further evidence of the band's musical leanings were gained during the tour when they were spotted in the crowd at a James Brown concert, giving it their all for the Godfather of Soul!

Inspired by this touring experience, Radiohead flew to LA in August to begin recording the album with Nigel Godrich. The location seemed rather glamorous for Radiohead, but as Jonny said, 'No, it's not very Radiohead, but we recorded the last album in a cold northern Europe location because we thought it was us. It wasn't. So we'll try this.' In fact, in terms of the musical experimentation for which Radiohead had become renowned, the Ocean Way studios in Hollywood were ideal for the band, being the site for the recording of classics by The Beach Boys, The Mamas and the Papas, and Frank Sinatra. Nigel Godrich also felt very at home there, as he had previously recorded at Ocean Way with Beck and Travis.

Until completion of recording in March 2003, Ocean Way became a nexus of operations for Radiohead. And this time, recording sessions went well. Journalists were amazed by the upbeat reports issuing from the studio, and cheekily ran articles with headlines such as 'Radiohead In "Happy" Shock'. By the autumn, Thom was pleased enough with the album's progress to speak to major music magazines about it, declaring that, 'we're working bloody hard on it now. We are trying to be a bit more focused, less neurotic'. He also indicated that the album would be 'the exact opposite of *Amnesiac* and *Kid A*' and that the summer tour and the recording sessions were all part of a plan 'to capture the whole performance thing, really; catching a particular moment. Because *Kid A* and *Amnesiac* were quite heavily thought through, we're trying to do the exact opposite of that.' However, he stressed that Radiohead were not rehashing the guitar sound of their early albums: 'That's the thing that would be a mis-

take to think; it's just sort of capturing that energy.' Radiohead's continued inventive-
ness was confirmed by reports Jonny posted on the Radiohead website describing an
array of instruments used in the album. One cheerful little note read, 'Played glock all
day . . . and guitar all yesterday. Kazoo tommorow.'

Indeed, Radiohead were successfully incorporating all the past lessons they had
learned about touring, recording and operating in the commercial arena, into a very
productive phase. Throughout 2002, they also held fast to their political ideals and
charitable principles. In April, Phil ran the London marathon to raise money for the
Samaritans, while in June Ed and Thom joined 100,000 people to protest outside
the Houses of Parliament for greater justice in global trade. Thom was passionate
about the issues at stake, telling reporters, 'I look at something like this as a starting
point. It's an awareness thing. Letting people know, 'this is being done in your
name, what are you going to do about it? I don't expect big things to happen. But I
do expect this government to take this with them when they go to the earth summit
and G8. These are economic issues but they have human and environmental conse-
quences.' The band also lent their suport to Friends Of The Earth in July, by donating

Some of the rhythms are definitely for shagging. If you like to shag very, very slowly. At 80bpm.'

a short Radiohead-produced film to the organisation. And Thom's charitable nature
propelled him to do a solo show in the US in October, as part of a benefit for children organised by one of Radiohead's heroes, Neil Young.

There were also some lighter moments for Radiohead in 2002. In the first half
of the year, Ed collaborated with Asian Dub Foundation on their new album. ADF
were delighted with the results, saying, 'It was an honour to have Ed play on the
album; we both have a great deal of admiration for each other's guitar styles. He's
got some wild sounds I can tell you!' Then in August, a surprising, but not very serious problem presented itself, when an old demo by the band surfaced on the
Internet. Containing songs recorded in 1991, the find caused great excitement
among fans. Despite the inferior quality of the recordings, the band made no
attempt to quash their circulation, and such was the interest in them that one fansite perpetually crashed due to the volume of traffic they generated. More silliness
was afoot in September when Thom and Colin attended a spoof awards ceremony
organised by the BBC's Mark and Lard, where the prize was a £25 clothing voucher.
A less dubious distinction then came in the form of the award for Best Act Act In

Thom Yorke is typically passionate in what turned out to be
an untypically lighthearted Radiohead set at Glastonbury 2003.

The World Today at the *Q* awards in October. And at the end of the year the band excelled themselves with a special Christmas webcast where they donned masks featuring the faces of George Bush, Tony Blair and Saddam Hussein, played records, and performed their new material, all a delight for fans.

The close of 2002 saw Radiohead looking to the future. They continued to divide their time between the US and the UK while they worked on the new album, but publicly declared that they would be touring in 2003. The general assumption was that the band would also headline Glastonbury, marking a return to the stage where they had made history five years previously . . .

'Radiohead will be completely unrecognisable in two years. At least I hope so.'

It was not until March 2003 that Glastonbury was given the go-ahead by the local council, the same month that Radiohead completed their new album. Up until then, the press reports circulating around the band were purely speculative, concentrating on possible album titles, and tracks for inclusion. Until shortly before the album's release the main title suggestions were *2+2=5* and *Are You Listening?* The release date was set for mid-June and a huge buzz of anticipation surrounded the band. This was reflected in the rapid ticket sales for a planned tour of small UK venues in May, which sold out within hours. Radiohead took this all in their stride. 'You know that time when bands begin to swagger', said Ed, 'like when the Stones got in a groove from '68-'73? In the last two years, I think we've done that.'

Then came the war with Iraq, which cast a shadow over everyone's lives. And the impending release of Radiohead's album placed them at the centre of the media response to events. In March, the band revealed that the new album would be entitled *Hail To The Thief* , this phrase taken from a slogan used by anti-George Bush protesters when he took power. The choice of title made it clear that Radiohead were anti-Bush and anti-war, a bold move for a band in their position. The announcement generated huge controversy. *NME* summed up the situation with the words, 'they have finally entered the protest with an elegant act of mainstream subversion which may yet prove to be the most radical statement made by a multi-platinum act, even at the potential cost of alienating their US fanbase and arousing media hostility.'

The move did cost Radiohead some fans. *NME* documented the deluge of emails the magazine had subsequently received, which revealed that the general opinion of

Radiohead was very divided. One email printed read, 'I believe in the US and have faith in my president. I think it's sad that this very talented band (perhaps the world's best) have gone from innovative lyrical and musical concepts to political protest.' The other, reflecting the polarised views, read, 'At a time when the ruling powers of the world have gone totally whack-o we need to be reminded of that fact by those we aspire to.'

However, the media furore made no difference to ticket sales for Radiohead's forthcoming live appearances. In fact the band took steps to stop touts profiting from fans desperate to acquire tickets for shows. The band arranged for anyone auctioning tickets on the web to have their orders cancelled, but tickets were still changing hands for hundreds of pounds. In April, the announcement of a full UK tour beginning in November provoked a similar stampede. And tickets for a Royal Festival Show in July sold out in less than half an hour, with 200 people turned away from the box office.

Fans may not have been able to get to the band, but they made sure they got to the music: on 30 March a copy of *Hail To The Thief* surfaced on the Internet, and was quickly downloaded and copied a thousand times over. Radiohead were understandably distressed and made their feelings clear on the band's website, pointing out that the version of the album was only a rough demo. Jonny spoke for all the band when he said, 'there's this, work we've not finished, being released in this sloppy way, ten weeks before the real version is even available. It doesn't even exist as a record yet . . . of course people will still download them and hear them, I can understand the temptation. It's not you lot I'm pissed off about, it's just the situation I guess. It's stolen work, fer fuck's sake.' Nigel Godrich was more succint: 'Hey listen, it's not that it's not mastered . . . It's not mixed! Some of it isn't even finished. Comprendez?'

However, it didn't take long for Radiohead to recognise the extent of interest in their unfinished work as a compliment, and even to see the funny side of the situation. The band were also bemused by the letters a panicked EMI were sending out to radio stations and websites, warning them not to play any of the rough tracks. 'Don't record companies usually pay thousands of dollars to get stations to play their records?', asked Colin. 'Now they're paying money to stations not to play them. It's all fucked. It's brilliant and it's terrible. It's a brave new world.' This relaxed attitude was becoming typical of 21st century Radiohead. And Colin's words were borne out, as the drama blew over with no serious commercial losses, in a matter of weeks. In April, radio stations began playing the first single to be officially released from the album, entitled 'There There'. It neatly encapsulates the tone of the album as a whole. Far from being a radio-friendly three minute pop song, it extended to five minutes in length and had no chorus, yet it also hailed the return of a more guitar-led sound. 'There, There' was a clear indication of Radiohead's intention to fuse their former brand of guitar rock with their new experimental work. It was proclaimed an instant classic by fans who fell in love with it, a sentiment echoed by Thom: 'I blubbed my eyes out. I went to LA and Nigel played me the mix and it just made me cry, I was in tears for ages, I just thought it was the best thing we had ever done.'

Hail To The Thief received mixed notices from the press, who got their hands on official preview copies of the album in May. Opinions ranged from disappointed to ecstatic. Chief source of disagreement was where in the Radiohead spectrum the album fell. Some critics lauded it as a triumphant return to guitar rock, albeit with a smattering of electronica, while others suggested that with *Hail To The Thief*, Radiohead had firmly entrenched themselves in the strange terrain of *Kid A* and *Amnesiac*. Fans were similarly divided, as Radiohead once again produced an album that, although brilliant, was difficult to pigeon-hole. However, *Hail To The Thief* went to number one in the album charts after its release in June 2003. Even the hardcore fans confounded all expectations when they rushed to buy another copy of the album from shops after downloading it from the Internet earlier in the year.

Hail To The Thief is a coda to *OK Computer, Kid A* and *Amnesiac*, rooted in Thom's concerns about the dark political forces that move in the shadows. It is neverthless not a political statement: 'With *Hail To The Thief*, the whole thing about it being political is a bit far-fetched', Thom told *Bang*, 'This record to me, these new songs, they're not so much songs about politics as me desperately struggling to keep politics out.' Thom had been deeply affected by the events of September 11, and the subsequent war and unrest. It was his inability to close his eyes or ears which created *Hail To The Thief*'s oblique politicism: 'There was this noise going round my house and it was the noise that ended up in the songs. This was during the Afghan war and stuff, and lots of it felt wrong. Everything felt wrong.' In order to avoid confusion, Thom went to great lengths to explain the lyrics in later interviews, and included them in the album's artwork.

The artwork itself reflects the multiple layers of meaning which Radiohead inserted. The cover features a rough roadmap of Hollywood, with different words written in each city block. According to Colin, 'the overall effect is designed to play up and point out the dynamics and dangers of consumerism.' Yet considering the album-title's reference to George Bush's allegedly stolen election victory, few could fail to spot the allusion to Bush's own roadmap: his plans for the middle east. When *NME* noted the similarity, Thom responded, 'ours is better. More coherent' – ironic, given how *Hail To The Thief*'s artwork was put together: Thom explained that he had been inspired by, 'listening to lots of Radio 4. Whenever I heard words that rang bells in my head, I'd write them down, until I had this really long list, which is basically much of the artwork.'

In terms of content, *Hail To The Thief* contains a dynamic mix of musical styles. Tracks such as 'There, There', '2+2=5', 'Scatterbrain' and 'Myxomatosis' and 'Go To Sleep' marked the anticipated return to a more conventionally guitar-based sound. '2+2=5' opens the album with a gently ominous guitar riff. Thom's plaintive vocals slide in, before the song breaks out into a riot of frantic guitar and punk posturing. It all ends as suddenly as it began. The next track, 'Sit Down, Stand Up', dispels any illusions that this album heralds a simple return to a pre-*Kid A* Radiohead. It was written after Thom had seen footage of Rwanda on television. With its minimalist lyrics, beats and melody, it was described by *Q* as 'dangerously close to being all experimentalism and precious little substance.' Yet the song's structure – its foreboding beginning, gradually building to an frenetic close – closely parallels that of '2+2=5'. It's as if the admittedly opaque lyrics are merely a red herring. 'Scatterbrain' is another pretty variation on the voice and guitar theme. The lyrics were conceived out of Thom's solitary ramblings through cities torn by foul weather. 'Myxomatosis', named after the rabbit disease, and derived from Amnesiac track 'Dollars and Cents' is an industrial assault of keyboards and guitars that had already met with a strong response when the band had played it live. The lyrics sound like a twisted account of Thom's career to date; one of the lines, 'No one likes a smart ass, but we all like stars,' neatly sums up his relationship with the press. At the other end of the scale 'Go To Sleep' is Radiohead with a folk inflection. Thom's vocals, accompanied by an acoustic riff, combine ominous lyrics with a melody which owes much to folk harmonies and inflection. The song's eclecticism is confirmed when a second guitar breaks out into clipped rock phrases. 'I Will', a hymn to Iraqi families vaporised during an accidental bombing during the first Gulf War, dates back to the *Kid A* sessions. Its lyrics are heavy with fear that the future will see no progress, yet the melody itself, with its gently strummed guitar and Thom's tired-sounding voice, is suggestive more of resignation than struggle.

Whereas 'Where I Begin And You Begin' combines energetic drums and bass with plaintive electronica to mourn the inevitability of human isolation, 'Backdrifts' and 'The Gloaming' lean toward Radiohead's more minimal electronic side. The technical knowledge gleaned from recording their previous albums is evident. 'Backdrifts' is a spartan but lovely piece of electronica, developed out of the band's early experiments with synthesisers, the original version written on a Q170 sequencer. Opening with percussive static and heart-beat bass over a back-drop of glitches, 'The Gloaming' evokes intense feelings of isolation and claustrophobia. It breaks out into a rash of electronic sounds like paranoid thoughts trapped in someone's head. The song is populated by haunting moans, and the constantly reiterated bass line fades in and out of audibility. In an interview with *NME*, Thom explained that he had often referred to the whole album as "The Gloaming", transposing the word for the ancients' vision of the twilight zone, where everything is shrouded in beautiful but terrible uncertainty, onto a modern idea of the world. 'I sound like a loony. But there's an awful lot of shadows and malignant forces that are pulling strings at the moment. It's barely human, it's something that's coming from somewhere else, and that is impossible to control . . . if you meet a powerful politician – it's like shaking hands with thin air. The tornado has nothing in the middle. The gloaming to me is exploring this unhealthy darkness, which it seems it's impossible to counteract.'

The album also contains tracks that even for Radiohead, are musical oddities, 'We Suck Young Blood' is a mournful dirge which briefly lapses into a musical frenzy. Thom has said of this track, 'For me that song is not to be taken seriously, but at the same time it was quite fun . . .' The track had serious undertones though, as Thom created it out of disgust at Hollywood celebrity. ('We Suck Young Blood' has formed the basis of a typically subversive poster campaign, which appeared to be an advert for a talent contest but was made up of song lyrics). 'A Punch Up At A Wedding' was also something of an unexpected turn, as Radiohead got quietly funky, with Thom meting out grooves on the piano.

'Sail To The Moon' can simply be filed under 'vintage Radiohead'. An exquisite ballad, it quickly became a crowd-pleaser on the band's summer 2002 tour. With its reference to 'an Ark', it has been suggested that the song is addressed to Thom's son, Noah. This transforms the song from a hauntingly beautiful but essentially empty meditation on responsibility and power to an exploration of guilt, failure and parental hope.

The album ends with 'A Wolf at the Door', the album's most vitriolic offering. Gentle guitar, bass and drums meander eerily through the song as we are bombarded with images of violence, loss and fear. The lyrics were inspired by ragga freestyling, constructed from the notebook of words and phrases Thom had been keeping while he worked on the album. 'A Wolf at the Door' is the song drawn most directly from the political noise going round Thom's house. It is the ragged summation of the dark influences which Thom distilled into the lyrics for the album – the politics bursting out in a wave of anger and frustration. As Radiohead would be the first to admit, it's just pop, but 'A Wolf at the Door', like the whole album, proves that pop can still be sophisticated, multi-layered and aware.

Thom left his sombre theorising behind for Radiohead's live dates in 2003. These began with a tour of small UK and Irish venues in May, the intimate gigs enjoyed as much by the band as the crowd. Aside from the buzz generated by Radiohead performing in small venues, another reason for the tour's success was that the band constantly varied their set, making each gig extra special. The June 28 return to Glastonbury was as triumphant as had been widely anticipated – taking the Pyramid Stage directly after the Flaming Lips, with whom the band had formed a mutual admiration society. Throughout the entire tour, Thom, much maligned as a 'miserabilist' in certain quarters, could be seen dancing wildly and grinning.

'The way the whole music scene is, it's getting more and more strange and we're finding it less easy to fit in.'

Hail To The Thief quickly became one of the year's best-selling albums in its country of origin, coming close to the quantities shifted of Coldplay's 2003 *A Rush Of Blood To The Head*. Apart from the release of their superlative new album, the biggest news surrounding Radiohead in 2003 was the launch of www.radiohead.tv, an online radio station all about the band. After fighting shy of the media, Radiohead had chosen to fight back via the Internet, the most potentially subversive form of communication, having already embraced it early on. 'Thom wants it to be called www.the-most-gigantic-lying-mouth-of-all-time.com,' one source close to the band told nme.com. But, for convenience, he was forced to adopt the more conventional title. 'Footage will include promo videos, webcast footage from live gigs as well as webcast footage from the studio. There are also a number of actual new Radiohead TV style programmes being put together which will be half an hour in length.'

The site was officially launched on 26 May with one such 30-minute show – preceded by snippets and tasters, including the promotional video for 'There There' on 10 May. Filmed in the 50 Acre Wood outside Bristol, the brief given by the band to director Chris Hopewell was 'a bit Brothers Grimm, a bit Jan Svankmajer' (the Czech director who made a wonderfully surreal animated film of Lewis Carroll's *Alice*). Thom's summation was typically deflating: 'It's *Bagpuss*.'

On hearing 'There There', Noel Gallagher told nme.com, 'I like it because it doesn't annoy me.' While it seemed like a backhanded compliment, he qualified it with, 'But then again with Thom Yorke and Jonny Greenwood in a band, they're going to be great, put them together and you've got genius.

'But I don't get the whole angst thing,' he complained. 'Radiohead have sold twenty million albums and they're still miserable?' (Or maybe it's just that they're sentient and sensitive human beings – factors that presumably never trouble the Gallagher brothers.)

By the time the band were about to start the US leg of the 2003 world tour, 'Go To Sleep' followed in quick succession as the second single from the album. Thom described the making of the video on www.radiohead.com: 'i had to wear the stupidest bobbly node suit. there were no cameras just infrared scanning light things. it was very strange. but oh yes thats me. i was mapped into it. from the movement data and hi res scans. much like TRON.' (*Tron* was the first 'virtual reality' film, made in the 1980s and set inside a video game.)

In November, Radiohead would follow up with a third single. '2+2=5' once again showed their musical eclecticism by backing the main tracks with remixes of 'Myxomatosis' by techno innovator Cristian Vogel and 'Scatterbrain' by Four Tet (aka DJ Kieran Hebden). '2+2=5' would prove the most popular of the album's single releases, going to number one in the *NME* chart for one week in November, before several weeks in the number two slot.

The US gigs were a particularly rare treat for longstanding American fans. Rarities in the set included 'Lurgee', the first track from *Pablo Honey* to be played in years, plus occasional covers of Neil Young's 'After the Gold Rush' (which Thom had first performed in 2001) and REM's 'Everybody Hurts'. (Thom would join REM onstage at an August Vancouver Thunderdome gig on 'It's The End Of The World As We Know It'.)

While not quite perceived as the Second Coming, the Oxford quintet's stateside return was seen by alt-rock fans as of great significance. As veteran rock critic Robert Christgau noted, 'upon those Oxonians now has fallen the dubious, dangerous mantle of Only Band That Matters'. '[Thom] smiled, he danced and the band whirled up a hurricane of sound. They proved that *Kid A* and *Amnesiac* are accessible and danceable,' enthused David Iskra in *Filter Magazine*, of a show at the Tweeter Centre in Camden, New Jersey. 'I promised myself I wouldn't write some cliched over the top "Radiohead Are Gods" article but that was before the show. If I wrote anything else I'd be lying.'

Part of the ecstatic audience response was doubtless due to the reappearance of 'Creep' in the set, after a long period of wilful neglect. 'It's quite difficult to play,' Colin told *Scotland on Sunday*, 'technically, not emotionally. But Thom's changed the lyrics. He always hated, "I want a perfect body, I want a perfect soul." Now it's, "I want a perfect body, to look good next to you."'

After two sell-out nights at the Hollywood Bowl in September, Thom also had the privilege of returning the following evening to introduce a hero of the band, far removed from all the cliched prog-rock associations. 'Somehow I have the pleasure of introducing,' he announced with apparent bewilderment, 'James Brown!'

One further departure took place at another end of the artistic spectrum. On 14 October, Radiohead appeared alongside Icelandic band Sigur Ros (whose ethereal mood music had earned comparisons with the Oxford quartet, as well as the unwelcome 'prog-rock' tag) at the Brooklyn Academy of Music, in the presence of New York City Mayor Michael Bloomberg. This unique event was entitled *Split Sides*, and was a performance by the Merce Cunningham Dance Company.

Cunningham, who began performing as a dancer himself in the late 1930s, is regarded as an artistic innovator whose avant-gardisms remain on the right side of accessibility. By now 84, and unaware of either band, Radiohead and Sigur Ros were recommended to him for the event by the general manager of his company. Interested in experimental music (he regularly collaborated with the legendary John Cage) and modern technology, Cunningham devised a novel premise for the performance: neither the dancers nor the bands would rehearse together – in fact, only the dancers would rehearse at all, choreographing their routine independently (and ultimately out of sync) with their musical accompaniment. Two pieces would be performed, at a duration of twenty minutes each, with the order of the dancers' and the bands' performances determined randomly by a roll of the dice.

As Jonny confirmed to *Billboard*, 'It was important to us and we took it seriously. It was a privilege. What a man! [Cunningham] is inspiring. We went to his apartment in New York and he was demonstrating how he used a laptop to do the choreography, and he's in his eighties. He sat there using a [Macintosh] G4. Just to have not given up and keep changing is inspiring.'

As Joan Acocella noted in the *New York Times*, 'the average age of Cunningham's audience seemed to have dropped by about 30 years'. Radiohead were decreed first on by the dice, setting the soundtrack for the dancers in their monochromatic black and white costumes. The band improvised a set of electronic music using keyboards, laptop computers and mixing desks. Thom's vocal performance was limited to wordlessly intoning into the mike as he turned knobs at the desk, just one more element in a mix which included synthetic string sounds, vocal sound effects and cut-ups of the voice of an American evangelist. According to *NME*, it was, 'Closer to *Kid A* than any other Radiohead material . . . unlike anything they've ever done, as they were essentially making it up as they went along.' Although both bands only performed live on the first night, their performances were taped and replayed over several subsequent evenings. For a major league band on a US tour, their artistic adventurousness was virtually without precedent.

Despite keeping average ticket prices to a reasonable $37, *Rolling Stone* estimate that Radiohead grossed $13 million on their US tour, selling a further 500,000 albums in the process. With the US under their belt, the world tour would continue at a steady pace, with European gigs seeing out the rest of the year and dates in Japan and Australia booked for April 2004. 'We'll finally finish in the spring,' Colin told *Scotland on Sunday*. 'Then we'll work on songs. The plan is try to record for the sake of the songs rather than the sake of an album – no deadline or anything, just having fun.'

By December, Thom's own retrospective view of 2003, the year that saw the release of *Hail To The Thief*, was that it had been a 'strange year'. (Colin's view was doubtless more positive, since his wife, literary author Mollie McGrann, had given birth to their first son that month.)

'When I was in school, the Pixies and REM changed my life.'

'Psychologically it's been kind of difficult,' reflected Thom. 'The way the whole music scene is, it's getting more and more strange and we're finding it less easy to fit in. We did sort of make an effort to be nice this time and we still managed not to fit at all.' In a world of ruthless careerists selling pre-packaged rebellion as rock 'n' roll, the sincerity, thoughtfulness and willingness to experiment that characterises Radiohead seemed to be coming from another planet.

In the New Year, the short Australian tour would be a triumph. National newspaper *The Age* described the spectacle of Radiohead's 26 April gig at the Rod Laver Arena: 'The ingenious technology framed a stage that seemed to have a consciousness of its own, like a malevolent spaceship. It went supernova during "The National Anthem", erupting into frantic strobes and scrolling neon stripes.'

Despite *Age Online* reviewer Michael Dwyer's cruel jibe at Thom's 'dance technique, harking back to the Ian Curtis School of Dance' (Joy Division vocalist Curtis was an epileptic), all that soured the Australian jaunt was the cancellation of a further date at the Laver Arena, due to throat problems experienced by Thom. It didn't stop the band making the 2004 Coachella festival in California, at the beginning of May. Following on from the reformed Pixies, featuring proto-grunge icons Frank Black and Kim Deal, Thom paid tribute. 'When I was in school, the Pixies and REM changed my life,' he affirmed during the encores, while others noted how Radiohead could have sold out the 50,000-capacity venue on their own, but felt privileged to share the stage.

The LA Times was just as enamoured of Radiohead's performance, musing, 'there is a sense of everyman in Yorke's vocals and a bold ambition in the band's lovely, often fragile arrangements that addresses cornerstone rock issues of self-affirmation and doubt with as much fervent emotion as almost anyone has brought to a stage.' It would be the only time the band took to a US stage during 2004.

Meanwhile, back home in England, Thom increasingly found himself taking on the role of political commentator. Although he claimed the title *Hail To The Thief* was *not* the appropriation of the 2000 presidential election pun it was perceived to be ('I keep reading stuff now about how this album is all about politics and anti-America,' he told *Bang Magazine*, 'just because of the title and one or two quotes I gave'), there was no doubt about where his political sympathies lay.

During the US tour, he'd written an article for the UK's liberal-left newspaper *The Guardian*, 'on my small soapbox in a hotel bathroom in Washington DC.' The subject was fair trade (or rather the lack of), and the moral imperative for the West to relieve the debt burden on the Third World. Describing the World Trade Organisation's panacea of liberalised international (or multinational) trading as 'like a bus full of religious lunatics rolling into town singing free trade songs and banging tambourines as war and famine break out and all about them turns to shit,' Thom was in a strident mood. Demanding corporate accountability and respect for international human rights, there was a slight tone of political disillusionment: 'When I got involved in Jubilee 2000, and tried to persuade governments, the IMF and the World Bank to cancel the unpayable debts it seemed like a reasonably fair thing to ask . . . . I didn't believe they would deny us. But they did.'

This spirit of wounded idealism found further voice in late November 2003, when President George W. Bush came to Britain on a state visit, ostensibly at the invitation of Buckingham Palace. Thom saw it rather differently, outraged that US secret servicemen were given permission to create a three-mile exclusion zone around the President in central London. While deemed necessary for security reasons, many saw it as simply a means to block protest against the Iraq War, and the role played by British troops at the behest of Tony Blair. For Thom, in particular, Iraq was a very sore point – not least because he'd originally accepted that the murderous Saddam Hussein provided the pretext for declaring war on his country. 'I bought it,' he morosely owned up to *The Guardian*. 'I thought, OK, if he has these weapons, they should be taken off him. You'd think I'd know better.'

Becoming increasingly overt in his anti-Bush sentiment, Thom admitted to some trepidation on the recent US tour. 'We were sort of worried about the reaction to what we had been saying when we went over there,' he admitted. 'Colin, whose wife is American, didn't see a problem at all. It turned out that he was right, when you met people face to face the resistance, disgust and dismay was obvious.

'When we played "No Surprises" a huge cheer would go up every night over the line "Bring down the government / They don't speak for us . . ." Although in Houston, Texas [home state of the President, where he formerly occupied the position of governor] it was a little err . . . muted shall we say.' Roused to indignation, Thom now emailed *NME* to urge the music community's performers and fans to make their voices heard.

Asked what purpose such an upsurge of opinion would serve, Thom asserted, 'To make Blair squirm over his decision to take us into an illegitimate war and follow this religious lunatic [Bush] toward a dangerous future for the whole planet.

'Both of these men are liars. We have the right to call them such; they are putting our children's future in jeopardy. They are not controlling the terrorist threat, they are escalating it. Blair will not be allowed off the hook by his pathetic pleading for us to "move on", neither shall Bush.'

Thom put much faith in the (supposedly independent) inquiry into the suicide of UK government weapons inspector Dr. David Kelly. Kelly had come under intense governmental and media pressure, after being revealed as the source for a BBC radio story that claimed the decision to go to war in Iraq was already taken, irrespective of whether Saddam allowed UN weapons inspectors to re-enter the country. According to the source, government spin doctors had 'sexed up' a dossier on alleged weapons of mass destruction to support the decision.

'As we are still awaiting the results of the Hutton inquiry I think now is a good time to remind Blair that he's on very, very, very, very, very, very, very, very thin ice,' announced Thom, with uncharacteristic bombast.

By the end of January 2004, however, an angry, downhearted Thom felt moved to pen another piece (entitled 'This Theatre of the Absurd') for *The Guardian*. 'When the Hutton report arrived this week . . . I expected, at the very least, a grovelling apology from Tony Blair. I had been looking forward to this for months.

'Instead, I have had to stomach the gloating and moralising of Blair, [Defence Secretary Geoff] Hoon and [spinmeister] Alastair Campbell as the establishment of this godforsaken country closes ranks to protect itself . . .'

Thom Yorke, as a well-educated, well brought-up middle-class boy, had allowed himself to believe that, if moral right was on his side, the truth would automatically out. The fact that the judge appointed to investigate by the government had cleared that same government of any wrongdoing was a bludgeoning disappointment. The only fault found was that of the BBC, held solely accountable for the situation that led Dr. Kelly to his death.

'Lord Hutton's damning report of the BBC is a whitewash,' accused Thom. 'The result will create fear at the *Today* programme, where there should be pride. As so many times before, they were there with a story that nobody else would touch . . .'

In the week of 29 December 2003 to 2 January 2004, Thom was able to demonstrate his loyalty to Radio Four's *Today* programme by sitting in as one of five guest editors drawn from various walks of British public life. Staying true to his own obsessions, he featured reports on music-making software and – naturally – on the suppressed pages of the US federal report into the 9/11 attacks. 'It was a great opportunity to get things said that aren't being said,' he explained. 'These are things that have occupied my mind all year so it's a chance to get someone else [i.e. BBC researchers] to do some work and find out things that I wanted to know about anyway.'

'We'd reached a point at the end of *OK Computer* when we were sick of that approach to song writing and we needed time away from it.'

Thom's wounded idealism was still undiminished in late September 2004, when he placed the following posting on the band website: 'i hope you all are well. it's saturday. i need to go to bed. im planning a trip to flyingdales anybody want to come? its a nice place, they have big domes and stuff. its up north. and im down south. bring a sandwich. i think they are planning world domination there or something.

'its the 25th. thats also a saturday. what should i say. i dont want to be rude. but they are about to announce star wars . . .' The so-called 'Star Wars' satellite defence system had been mooted since the presidency of Ronald Reagan in the 1980s, and now, under President Bush, Jr., was becoming a reality. Ostensibly the Star Wars strategy seemed benign – a defensive system which would enable the West to deflect attack by intercontinental ballistic missiles by zapping them from outside the earth's atmosphere. It was on this basis that the British government had, once again, put its defence facilities at the service of the US. But the organisers of the protest, the Yorkshire branch of CND (Campaign for Nuclear Disarmament), saw it as something more sinister, a potential system of attack allowing the USA to maintain its unchallenged single superpower status.

'How dare Tony Blair sign us up to "Star Wars" without even giving it a really serious thought . . . without even consulting us,' railed Thom before a crowd of just under 400 at the RAF Flyingdales Warning Base, where he had been invited to address the rally. 'It's sickening. It's important that people like us can get off our backsides and come to these events. We need to make it clear that we will not let America govern the world we live in.'

Even in the face of the reality of American military power, Thom quixotically refused to be cowed. As for the rest of the band, they continued to express their social conscience in a less confrontational manner. The 23 May 2004 performance by Ed, Colin and Phil – backing actor Bill Nighy on a cover of the Troggs' 'Love Is All Around', as he previously sang in *Love Actually* – was in aid of Helen House, Britain's first children's hospice. In November, Thom and Jonny joined engineer Nigel Godrich and a massed rank of prominent British rock stars (including Chris Martin of Coldplay and Fran Healy of Travis) for the third recording in two decades of the charity record 'Do They Know It's Christmas?' All profits, as ever, were to be channelled toward the horrifically impoverished of Africa. At the end of that same month, Thom took part in a sticky photoshoot to raise awareness on behalf of the fair trade movement. Doused in yucky-looking chocolate syrup, the gesture was intended to highlight how Third World farmers are 'dumped on' by the powerful industries of the West. It all put the lie to those who tried to stereotype Radiohead as gloomy, navel-gazing solipsists.

Despite their unease about the worsening international political situation, 2004 was in many ways a good year for Radiohead – despite the fact that relatively little was heard from them as a cohesive musical unit. In February, they won two of the most prominent annual *NME* Awards: best album for *Hail To The Thief,* and best video for 'There There'. Though, as the band ironically pointed out, the video was sole- ly the work of the filmmakers.

On 27 May, at a plush ceremony at central London's Grosvenor House, Radiohead won one of the British music industry's traditional Ivor Novello Awards for songwriting, in their specific case for International Achievement. Jonny told the UK's Teletext service, 'It's good that the Ivor's recognise writing. That's where it all starts, experimenting, making mistakes, breathing new life into what we do.'

But perhaps the most direct tribute came from the readers of *Q,* who, in the May 2004 issue, voted Radiohead's 1997 Glastonbury performance as the Greatest Gig of All Time – a true triumph snatched from the jaws of defeat, when the band were embattled by wind, rain, mud and the threat of electrocution.

Their only release as a band in 2004, *Com Lag,* had its title derived from Thom's fascination with Scientology, and its esoteric 'science' of Dianetics (though he's too independently minded to become a convert). The phrase means the time taken between the expression of a statement or problem, and its direct answer – to live better, according to Scientology, we must strive to eliminate much of the com lag in our lives.

An EP officially released in Japan only, *Com Lag*, a compilation of Radiohead's idiosyncratic and adventurous B-sides, sold well on import and online to the rest of the world. *NME* were enthused enough by it to offer a retrospective assessment of Radiohead's career: 'Never content with relaxing into an accepted way of doing things, this record, while being flawed . . . confirms that it's Radiohead rather than Oasis who are the true inheritors of the Beatles' legacy.'

Entering a more relaxed period of personal experimentation, Jonny Greenwood struck off on his own. Jonny had already introduced the strangely unique tones of the ondes martenot into the Radiohead sound: a cross between a keyboard and stringed instrument, he first heard it at school when his teacher played him some music by the twentieth-century French composer Messiaen. When he eventually came across one in a music shop in Paris, he bought it straight away. As he describes it, 'It looks like a tiny piano, and it's similar to the theremin, but more precise' – evoking the early electronic instrument featured on the soundtrack of classic sci-fi film *Forbidden Planet*. Its close cousin, the ondes martenot, is, as Jonny explains, the instrument that makes 'that swirly sound like a woman's voice on the *Star Trek* theme'.

Jonny incorporated his love of the esoteric instrument into a composition called 'Smear', which received its premiere via the London Sinfonietta as part of the city of Leeds' Fuse Festival at the West Yorkshire Playhouse, on 3 March 2004. Critical responses were positive, to say the least. *The Guardian* described 'Smear' as 'an ambient ripple of a piece from Radiohead's Jonny Greenwood, [which] provided glimpses of exquisitely sumptuous textures where its predecessor had been raw, and . . . deployed ondes martenots . . . that often suggested birds trying to sing synthesiser music.' *The Financial Times*, of all papers, was even more enthusiastic: 'Emitting a subtle radiance, based on mystic, Messiaenesque meditation one moment and quasi-futuristic motifs the next, "Smear" reveals an ear for timbre, a gift for musical elaboration and a more sophisticated palette than anyone might have guessed. Greenwood is clearly a composer in the making.'

Then came a solo album – not the launch of a career as a solo artist, but the soundtrack to an art movie. As Jonny put it to *Billboard*, 'There doesn't seem to be a point in doing a bad indie album with me trying to sing on top. That would be terrible for everybody.'

Bodysong, directed by Simon Pummell, is an almost hallucinatory documentary montage of images, comprised of a mass of material found everywhere from news archives to out-of-copyright feature films. Released in December 2004, its theme was nothing less than the physical 'experience of being human', from birth to death, taking in the fundamental human traits of sex and violence along the way.

'It was done in the same studio [as Radiohead],' confirmed Jonny to *The Independent*, 'with all the same instruments lying around, and some of the techniques we learnt for those albums are reproduced here, I'm sure. There was a lot of music to provide: the film doesn't have any dialogue in it, just music and images for an hour and twenty minutes . . . . I could just do three or four minutes of music in whatever mood, and people could play in free time – and occasionally, Simon Pummell would even edit the film to the length of the music, which was a real luxury.'

Film excerpts – including vintage erotica, or the infamous footage of a South Vietnamese colonel shooting a Viet Cong suspect through the head – were run side by side. Like a cinematic counterpart of musical samples, they were given renewed power by their new context.

And by their powerful soundtrack. *Bodysong*, the album, was released on Parlophone/EMI in the UK on 27 October. Recorded by Jonny and Graeme Stewart, its eclectic, part-electronic, part-acoustic soundscapes also featured contributions by the Emperor String Quartet, a jazz quartet led by saxophonist Gerrard Presencer, and Colin Greenwood on occasional bass.

Hartley Goldstein waxed lyrical in his pitchforkmedia.com review: 'The album's opener, "Moon Trills", marries pensive and melancholy piano chords reminiscent of Radiohead's "Pyramid Song" with swarming frenetic string swells, and weepy ondes-martenot accompaniment. The only aspect of *Bodysong* that's somewhat disappointing is the inconspicuous lack of guitar work . . . . This fact may be of little surprise given that Radiohead themselves have infamously eschewed guitars in favour of other musical approaches.'

None the more for that, Jonny regarded it as strictly a one-off. 'You realise quite quickly how good it is to be in a group,' he told nme.com. 'Thom was suggesting titles for things and everyone in the band had a two CD version and helped me whittle it down to half the length.' Appreciative of the group input, Jonny concluded of his solo work, 'I think I'd only do it again if everyone else wanted to stop.'

But there was more in the pipeline than Jonny's self-deprecating attitude let on. Later in the year, the *Sunday Times* printed the intriguing news that he had been commissioned by the BBC as composer in residence for its Radio Three station. His three-year appointment by station controller Roger Wright was as replacement for the previous incumbent, classical musician Anne Dudley. According to Wright, 'the great joy about this deal is that Jonny is not a classical composer. He has a great talent and we want to give him the opportunity to simply be creative. We want him to try things out with brass and string, to experiment. Anything goes and we are all enormously excited.'

'It's insane,' enthused Jonny to *The Guardian*, 'because I've got a whole orchestra to myself. I still can't believe it. It's that thing of standing in a quiet room, and experiencing the way the air moves when the orchestra starts to play. It's so seductive.'

His new commission entailed writing original pieces for live and recorded performance, even creating radio theme tunes. Whilst establishment critics like the *Sunday Telegraph*'s Michael White denounced Jonny's appointment as 'very questionable', he geared up for his first concert in April 2005 with the BBC Concert Orchestra. This was immediately preceded by a further performance with the London Sinfonietta at the 2005 Ether Festival on the South Bank, over the Easter weekend. As both performer and curator, his programme featured a revised version of 'Smear', a new Greenwood original, 'Piano For Children', and pieces by his favourite modern classical composers, Krzystof Penderecki (whose sinister strings adorn *The Exorcist*'s soundtrack), Messiaen and Gyorgy Ligeti.

'Growing a beard and starting to bake your own bread and stuff has made me realise that maybe I'm not right all the time.'

But most significant, as far as Radiohead fans were concerned, was the appearance of Thom Yorke to perform (along with Jonny and the Nazareth Orchestra) a new song entitled 'Arpeggi'. Derived from the plural of the Italian musical term 'arpeggio', meaning the rapid plucking of individual chords, the song was described as a subtle, beautifully orchestrated piece with similar vocals to 'How To Disappear' or 'Pyramid Song'. Thom read his atmospheric lyrics from a sheet, about being metaphorically 'at the bottom of the ocean', while Jonny augmented the orchestra on ondes martenot. They also performed a revised version of 'Where Bluebirds Fly', complete with Arabic inflexions to the music and a duet between Thom and female vocalist Lubna Salame.

'We haven't started manipulating sounds of orchestral instruments,' an enthusiastic Jonny said to *Computer Music Journal* of his regular work with the band. 'I just feel that there are still so many sounds and textures to get out of orchestras that are unlike anything, and can be far more disturbing/magical than most digital manipulation . . . microtonal string music and choirs and suchlike are far more affecting to me, because it's simultaneously natural and unnatural. As a band we listen to a lot of Penderecki.'

'Radiohead is always going to be the centre of what I do,' he told *The Guardian* at the time of the Ether concerts. 'We're rehearsing at the moment, and again it's fun. We all want to push forward, and when you have five people who are all like that, you couldn't ask for a better thing.'

As to how his whirlwind series of musical collaborations had prepared him for a return to the group fold, he opined, 'I'll be able to bang on with more confidence about whatever instrument happens to be obsessing me at the moment. Yesterday I was trying to explain how we have to get hold of a clavichord.'

As far as the future of Radiohead was concerned, on the eve of the first Ether concert Jonny had posted an official website message: 'we're all kind of "hungry" for new new new at the moment.'

Thom continued to evince steely determination. Having previously claimed, 'Radiohead will be completely unrecognisable in two years,' he told the Associated Press in 2004, 'We feel that after *Hail To The Thief* we want to definitely disappear into a black hole of the unknown rather than carrying on where we left off.'

'The lows are when you are like litmus paper: you absorb more when everything is twice as loud and everything is twice as bright.'

Indeed, he wouldn't even commit himself to the idea of another full-length CD. 'It's always been album, album, album,' he complained, speaking positively of the technology that more conservative figures saw as the death of the recording industry. 'Things like iTunes and people splitting up tracks, I kind of think that's good. I listen to music on random all the time.'

When quizzed by Virgin Radio at the 2004 *NME* Awards about the proximity of a new release, Thom had answered, 'Not doing a new album. Because we're out of contract [with EMI], so we go in our studio and make some stupid noises and then . . . You,' he addressed Jonny, 'go in on Mondays. Phil's got Thursdays. Sometimes we share on Fridays. I'm in on Tuesdays and Wednesdays.'

When the band went into hiatus in mid-2004, Phil told Teletext, 'It's not very rock and roll, but we all have families, so we'll be with them until at least the end of summer. We need to press the reset button on everything before we work out what to do next. We've no new songs, not one.'

As he later told *NME*, 'We'd reached a point at the end of *OK Computer* when we were sick of that approach to song writing and we needed time away from it. We don't think we feel that way now. I don't think we need to knock down what we've done before and completely reinvent ourselves but at the same time we need to improve as musicians, we need new material, and to try arrangement ideas.'

As the band's visibility receded, Radiohead TV, which initially seemed such a radical idea, was taken offline. This was before the scheduled Episode Four of their half-hour TV series could be shown. 'We were going to take over the airwaves,' Thom announced in a rather forlorn website announcement dated 2 September. 'So we set about puxing together some television. We got lots of tapes from a request we put on our website. Lots. Lots and lots . . . . [Then] Something about money, cutbacks, too weird, might scare the children, staV layoVs, shareholders . . . It was a shame considering there is a lot of people's hard work here.' By December, however, a DVD entitled *The Most Gigantic Lying Mouth Of All Time* was released, featuring all four of the composite web shows.

The recording of a much-anticipated new album was a process that would lay claim to most of 2005. In terms of musical input, Jonny's eclectic musical activities would have much more of an influence this time. 'It's actually a lot more healthy now, democracy wise, than it used to be,' Thom told rock critic Stephen Dalton. 'Partly because I was so paranoid and uptight about not getting my own way. Growing a beard and starting to bake your own bread and stuff has made me realise that maybe I'm not right all the time.'

In the interim, certain personal demons had also been, if not vanquished, then held at bay in a way that could only aid creativity. In an interview with the *Sydney Morning Herald* during the Australian tour, Thom described how the bipolar depression he suffers from 'is debilitating and sort of destructive but I don't consider that I'm in any way unusual. I consider that I'm very lucky because I have a way of dealing with it, which is working . . . . The lows are when you are like litmus paper: you absorb more when everything is twice as loud and everything is twice as bright.

'I got back into drawing,' the former art student explained of how he was coping with the manic highs and depressive lows. 'Lots of drawing, and lots of walking. It was the best help I could get, really, especially the extreme weather and strong winds and things like that. It kind of reflects what's going on inside.'

But Thom has never been subdued enough by his depression to retreat from the world. The international political issues that he cares about continue to galvanise him into action. On 15 April 2005, he joined 25,000 people outside Whitehall, the centre of parliamentary government in London, to protest about the issue of fair trade in the Third World. The campaign was organised by War On Want and the Trade Justice Movement, to whom Thom lends his support. Speaking out after a one-minute silence at midnight, Thom told nme.com, 'It is important to remind

Blair and [Chancellor] Gordon [Brown] of their promises really. They are talking the whole thing up and they are on the [General Election] campaign trail and [fair trade] is one of the many things we are hassling them about.'

The campaign's roster of events included two such vigils, a five-hour painting 'performance' (with participation by Radiohead album cover designer Stanley Donwood) – and a rare solo acoustic performance of Radiohead songs by Thom, performed at about 3 a.m. for around 200 spectators. The five-song set was comprised of 'an old song which has never seen the light of day' called 'Glass Flowers', new song 'House Of Cards', plus the little-performed 'Nude', 'No Surprises' from *OK Computer* and new song 'Reckoner'.

By the beginning of the following month, Radiohead had regrouped for rehearsals on their new material – and, ultimately, their new album. 'It's going well,' Thom told nme.com in early May. 'It's a bit like *Kid A* – we're going through a period of change. But that's good. We'll get there.' Songs that made the shortlist included the new numbers previewed at the fair trade rally, and 'Arpeggi'. Also mooted were the new songs performed during the 2004 live dates, 'I Froze Up', 'Good Morning Mr. Magpie' and 'Up On The Ladder'.

Refusing to be limited by the success of what came before, or even by the technology the band sometimes seem in thrall to, Thom described the musical evolution of Radiohead as an organic process. 'Since we started making records, they've coincided with our discovery of new musical genres,' he mused to *Bang Magazine*. 'Each time you get into some other area of music you've never been in before, you realise the sky is the limit. You go, "Fuck, this exists too!" . . . . Each time you discover something new, you realise that what you've been doing thus far really means so little, is really so small a portion of all possible musics.'

Jonny had his own personal take on it. 'I think it would be awful if I started thinking, "Let's mix this with this, 'cause I like them both,"' he told *Filter Magazine*, before coming closer to Thom's point of view. 'But then, you know, we tend to kind of record something – with Radiohead, anyway . . . – and one of us will say, "Oh, it would be great if this had the texture of an Alice Coltrane record," or whatever. And so we'll try and do that.'

On 16 August 2005, www.radiohead.com opened a new weblog journal entitled Dead Air Space. The first part of the blog came from Thom, under a heading that evoked a classic Talking Heads album by asking, 'DO YOU HAVE "FEAR OF MUSIC"?' 'is anybody in there?' the blog began. 'personally it has taken a long time to get my CONFIDENCE BACK. after getting a kicking although it wasnt a kicking. was it? commercial suicide. and proud of it. but it wasnt. just a little stink bomb at a lousy party.'

It seemed a little neurotic, almost a cry for help. But there was something more positive in the offing, as the next day's posting almost intimated: 'we have no record contract as such. any offers? . . . what we would like is the old EMI back again. the nice genteel arms manufacturers who treated music [as] a nice side project who werent to bothered about the shareholders.'

Ironic as the reference to his former corporate bosses and their weapons division was, on 21 August Thom placed the following posting: 'hello good people its sunday august 21 2005 and we're recording .... let me fill you in a little. so apart from a 3 and half week tour to the other side of the world in april of 2004 the rest of that year was a dormant one for us .... we needed a break .... the end of another 3 album cycle .... they're not planned like that but thats how it seems to be . . . so we reconvened in mid-february and since then we've been trying to kick start the old beast . . . so here we are in the recording studio and it feels right. its only day 4. its very early days but really good things are happening .... lots of deconstructing and reassembling. we've been working on mornin' m' lud and pigsee.'

Thom also told the fanbase that Colin was playing 'sleaz bass' on 'Morning M'Lud', which sounded like a 'freight train', and that they were ensconced in a remote rural setting where they spent their downtime 'going out on bikes up hill with no gears'.

'Each time you get into some other area of music you've never been in before, you realise the sky is the limit. You go, "Fuck, this exists too!"'

Jonny's posting on Friday 23 September was altogether more laidback, focusing on the eclectic guitarist/composer's current musical fixation: '. . . I choose reggae because I know so many people who collect this kind of music and no other – which fascinates me – and because it's mostly unknown to me. Not any more . . . I've just done it. Six solid months of nothing but Lee "Scratch" Perry, Ken Boothe, Junior Byles, Marcia Atkin and hundreds of others. It's to make a compilation which may or may not ever be completed – I hope I'm not just proving a point to myself – but either way, there's been nothing else on my ipod since April.' (Fittingly, the Easy Star All-Stars, the collective who recorded *Dub Side Of The Moon*, the underground dub reggae take on Pink Floyd's classic *Dark Side . . .*, are planning a reggae version of *OK Computer* for September 2006 release.)

Characteristically, Thom's entry for that day was angst-ridden in comparison: 'i could write about how im finding it difficult to finish lyrics. that there are giant waves of self doubt crashing over me and if i could alleviate this with a simple pill

. . . i think i would

'although it is a necessary part of the procedure.'

As the weeks wore on and the band's collective creativity picked up, so it seems did Thom's spirits. On 28 September, he was able to write, 'im working on something that i think is called PAY DAY. im gonna lay the lyrics line by line on the floor and shuffle them. and im having to play gentle fingerpicking over furious beat.' He also spoke of a track potentially entitled 'Burn The Witch' (or 'Burn The White Witch'), observing, 'jonny has lots of orchestration tasks now including this...("oh good" says he exiting stage left).'

But, even in their rural musical retreat, the outside world could still intrude. 'friends of the earth have asked me whether i would meet Tony Blair at downing street to discuss what our government is not doing about climate change.' Even though his current agenda was strictly musical, Thom's environmental conscience was pricked. 'i don't know if this will ever happen for certain . . . it is rattling around in the back of my mind and concerns me a lot. i have no intention of being used by spider spin doctors to make it look like we make progress when it is just words.'

As the autumn wore on, the band's productivity seemed to inspire a greater optimism. 'yet another new tune added to the blackboard called Rubbernecks,' Thom confirmed on 11 October, quoting its lyric: 'its coming up the drive / rubbernecks with cameras / petrol and bonfires (heres the loud bit) / we need to keep away the rubbernecks.'

On 22 October, Ed O'Brien observed, 'the dogs have gone to bed . . .

'friday night …….. the end of a two week session …….. riffs and fragments of the songs going round my head …….. its been great ……..its always difficult to judge right now but i think we may have got "bodysnatchers"' But Thom, of course, was less happy-go-lucky. 'bananas,' he announced, 'it is the end of our two week session. were splitting up its all shit. were washed. up. finished.'

Then, backtracking with an 'only kidding', his mood lightened considerably: '. . . there were moments that stick in my head when I went "TUNE!" "TUNE!" like tonight listening through "house of cards." its us, no denying it. but thats cool. i like it. it has its own power. cant fight that i suppose. although i see it as my duty to try.'

In the wake of the recording sessions, one of the final postings (dated 28 November) on Dead Air Space confirmed that, however uplifting an experience the new album had turned out to be, Thom's angst about the state of the world remained undiminished: 'so the UN are meeting in Montreal to decide what to do after the Kyoto protocol [on global warming]. and already the US administration has buried its witless head in the fucking sand. refusing to take part. you can even see the strings being pulled. this is a true evil.'

As the 21st century passed into the middle of its first decade, Radiohead remained at the forefront of popular culture. *Q* magazine, which had already cited their Glastonbury '97 performance as the Greatest Gig of All Time, printed their readers' poll to find the Greatest Album of All Time in their January 2006 edition. At the number one position, acclaimed as the greatest album ever, was *OK Computer*. At number two was *The Bends*. Further down the top ten came *Kid A*. It was a remarkable achievement, overshadowing the popularity of any other band in the 50-year history of rock music.

'Well, it's true, none of us are brilliant musicians, with the possible exception of Jonny. . . And I like the fact that we're not.'

Also at this time (late December 2005), two demo tapes became available online from the band's very earliest days as On A Friday. The first dated from 1988, containing the tracks 'Happy Song', 'To Be A Brilliant Light' and 'Sinking Ship'; the second originated from summer 1990, with fifteen familiar sounding track titles, all previously registered for copyright with Warner/Chappell in 2003: 'Climbing Up A Bloody Great Hill'; 'Somebody'; 'Mr B'; 'What's That You See?'; 'Everyone Needs Someone To Hate', 'Give It Up' and 'Rattlesnake' (these three representing Radiohead's first experiments with technology – with Thom recording drum loops off his Walkman from Public Enemy and Soul II Soul CDs, without the aid of a sampler); 'Upside Down'; 'The Greatest Shindig Of The World' (recorded here by Thom solo, with a change of chorus this became 'Maquiladora' on *The Bends*); 'How Can You Be Sure?' (another blueprint for *The Bends*); 'Life With The Big F'; 'Keep Strong'; 'Burning Bush' (an acoustic take of an early anti-Bush [Sr.] political polemic); 'Tell Me Bitch', and 'New Generation' (with ranting, semi-spoken vocals by Colin).

Historically, the demos became a source of fascination for any true Radiohead fan. But, in terms of significance, they didn't detract from the sense of anticipation that surrounds the 2006 release of the band's new music. Ultimately, the greatest hope for the future of Radiohead is expressed by Thom Yorke – in terms of the future's lack of certainty. 'Well, it's true, none of us are brilliant musicians, with the possible exception of Jonny,' he self-deprecatingly claims. 'And I like the fact that we're not. And it's good to have our doubts about . . . everything . . . . Our attitude about music is: "I don't know." Well, let's find out.'

CREDITS

The following journalists, articles, publications, radio stations, television shows and Internet publications proved invaluable in producing this book, and provide excellent sources for all fans. The author would like to express his thanks for their work: *NME*, 17/1/98 live review: David Fricke; *Rolling Stone*, 7/97 album review: Mark Kemp; *Melody Maker*, 13/6/92 live review: Ian Gittens; *Melody Maker*, 11/3/95 feature: Stud Brothers; *Melody Maker*, 6/5/95 live review: Neil Kulkarni; *Melody Maker*, 4/9/93 live review: Dave Jennings; *Melody Maker*, 2/7/94 live review; *Melody Maker*, 26/8/95 single review: Paul Lester; *Melody Maker*, 8/5/93 single review; *Melody Maker*, 4/9/93 single review; *Melody Maker*, 25/2/95 single review; *NME*, 18/3/95 album review: Mark Sutherland; *NME*, 18/3/95 feature: Simon Williams; *NME*, 23/10/93 live review: Randee Dawn; *NME*, 13/7/96 live review: Mark Beaument; *NME*, 26/8/95 single review; *NME*, 2/7/94 live review: John Harris; *Melody Maker*, 31/7/93 live review: Jon Wiederhorn; *Melody Maker*, 9/5/92 single review; *Melody Maker*, 14/8/93 feature; *NME*, 8/10/94 live review: Paul Moody; *NME*, 4/6/94 live review: Simon Williams; *NME*, 25/2/95 live review: John Harris; *NME*, 30/5/92 feature: Simon Wiliams; *Esquire*, 9/97 feature: Adam Sweeting; *Q*, 6/97 feature: Tom Doyle; *Q*, 10/97 feature: Phil Sutcliffe; *Mojo*, 9/97 feature: Jim Irvin; *Record Collector*, 11/96 feature: Pat Gilbert; *NME*, 27/5/95 feature: Ted Kessler; *NME*, 11/12/93 live review: Dele

Fadele; *NME*, 25/2/95 single review; *NME*, 7/6/97 live review: Ted Kessler; *Melody Maker*, 23/1/93 live review: Peter Paphides; *Melody Maker*, 10/10/92 feature: Dave Jennings; *Melody Maker*, 9/5/92 feature: John Harris; *Melody Maker*, 6/2/93 feature: Peter Paphides; *Melody Maker*, 11/9/93 live review: Chris Roberts; *Melody Maker*, 25/2/95 live review: David Bennun; *Melody Maker*, 21/10/95 live review: Andrew Meuller; *Melody Maker*, 20/5/95 single review; *Melody Maker*, 8/10/94 live review: Ian Watson; *Melody Maker*, 28/10/95 feature: Andrew Mueller; *NME*, 22/5/93 live review: Johnny Cigarettes; *NME*, 28/6/97 feature: Stuart Bailie; *Melody Maker*, 8/4/95 live review: Andrew Meuller; *Melody Maker*, 1/10/94 feature: Jennifer Nine; *Melody Maker*, 23/10/93 feature: Paul Lester; *Melody Maker*, 24/5/97 feature: Mark Sutherland; *NME*, 13/9/97 live review: Stephen Dalton; *NME*, 1/10/94 feature: Stuart Bailie; *Melody Maker*, 31/5/97 feature: Mark Sutherland; *Melody Maker*, 23/1/93 single review; *Melody Maker*, 10/6/95 feature: Caitlin Moran; *NME*, 4/9/93 single review; *Melody Maker*, 13/9/97 live review: Robin Bresnark; *NME*, 9/12/95 feature: Andy Richardson; *NME*, 3/9/94 live review; *Melody Maker*, 8/11/97 live review: Sharon O' Connell; *NME*, 11/9/93 feature: Paul Moody; *NME*, 27/2/93 live review: Paul Moody; *NME*, 10/10/92 feature: John Harris; *NME*, 30/1/93 single review; *NME*, 27/1/96 single review; *NME*, 13/12/97 feature: Ted Kessler;

NME, 29/11/97 live review: John Robinson; *Melody Maker*, 22/11/97 feature: Mark Roland; *NME*, 21/6/97 feature: Stuart Bailie; *NME*, 13/2/93 feature: Stuart Bailie; *Melody Maker*, 15/5/93 feature: Peter Paphides; *Melody Maker*, 11/6/94 feature: Holly Barringer; *Melody Maker*, 22/4/95 feature: Tom Doyle; *Melody Maker*, 20/2/93 album review: Andrew Meuller; *NME*, 20/2/93 album review: John Harris; *Melody Maker*, 18/5/96 live review: The Stud Brothers; *Melody Maker*, 11/6/94 live review: Dave Jennings; *Melody Maker*, 15/5/93 live review: Ian Gittens; *Melody Maker*, 24/5/97 feature; *NME*, 18/9/93 live review: John Harris; *NME*, 12/8/95 news; *NME*, 4/12/93 feature; *NME*, 12/9/92 live review: Simon Williams; *Spin*, 5/96 feature: J.D. Considine; *Shift magazine*, 6/96 feature; *The Orange County Register*, feature: Mark Brown; *Raygun*, 8/96 feature; *Curfew*, 12/91 feature: Ronan (Radiohead's first ever interview); *Addicted To Noise*, the on-line rock & roll magazine (www.addict.com) 1/8/97 news, 12/8/97 news: Micah Robinson; *Guitar World*, 10/97 feature: Bob Gulla; *MSN Music Central*, 8/97 feature; *Humo*, 22/7/97 feature; *Globe & Mail*, 25/6/97 feature: Elizabeth Benzetti; *Nightline (NZ)*, 6/97 TV interview; *Irish Times*, 17/5/97 feature: Kevin Courtney; *The Guardian*, 16/5/97 feature: Caroline Sullivan; *VOX*, 6/96 feature: Sam Steele; *VOX*, 7/97 feature with Thom Yorke; *Varsity*, 16/4/96 feature: Tojvo Pajo; *NME*, 10/10/95 live review: Angela Lewis; *NME*, 18/11/95 news; *Request*, 5/96 feature;

RAW, magazine 6/96 feature; *Rolling Stone*, 7/9/95 feature: John Wiederhorn; *Smug*, 8/96 feature: Shirley Halperin; *The Worcester Phoenix*, 4/7/97 feature: Ted Drozdowski; *The Diamond-back*, 15/4/96 feature; *Select*, 1/98 feature: John Harris; *Rolling Stone*, 25/12/97 feature: David Sinclair; *Spin*, 1/98 feature: Pat Blashill; *The Guardian*, 20/12/97 feature; *Select*, 11/97 live review: Roy Wilkinson; *Total Guitar*, 11/97 feature; *Rolling Stone (Australia)*, 10/97 feature: Cameron Adams; *The Web*, 11/97 feature: Adin Vaziri; *Spin On-line*, 9/97 feature: Roger Scott; *Indiana Daily Student*, 9/97 feature; *The New Yorker*, 24/9/97 feature: Alex Ross; *Spin*, 10/97 live review; *Select*, 7/95 feature; *Exclaim!*, 7/97 album review: James Keast; *Bang*, 07/04, feature: Neil Kulkarni and Emma Morgan; *Blender*, 06/01, feature; *Juice*, 10/00, feature; *LA Times*, 20/08/00, feature: Steve Hochman; *Melody Maker*, 20/09/00, feature: Mark Beaumont; *Mojo*, 06/01, feature; *Mojo*, 6/03, album review: Peter Paphides; *NME*, 03/05/03, feature: John Robinson; *NME*, 03/08/02, feature: Johnny Davis; *NME*, 04/01/03, feature: Julian Marshall; *NME*, 05/04/03, news feature: Stephen Dalton; *NME*, 10/05/03, feature: John Robinson; *NME*, 24/06/00, live review; *Q*, 04/01, feature; *Q*, 05/01, album review: Danny Eccleston; *Q*, 05/01, single review: Dorian Lynskey; *Q*, 06/12/00, feature; *Q*, 07/03, album review: John Harrise; *Q*, 07/03, feature: Michael Odell; *Q*, 08/01, single review: Dorian Lynskey; *Q*, 10/00, feature:

Danny Eccleston; *Q*, 10/01, album review: Stuart Maconie; *Record Collector*, 11/00, feature; *Rolling Stone*, 00, album review: David Fricke; *Rolling Stone*, 21/06/01, album review: Jon Pareles; *Rolling Stone*, 22/11/01, album review: Tom Moon; *Rolling Stone*, 24/10/03, feature: Jason Cohn and Michael Krugman; *Rolling Stone*, 26/6/03, album review: Toure; *Rolling Stone*, 5/5/01, feature: David Fricke; *Spin*, 04/01, feature; *Telegraph Magazine*, 05/03, feature: Craig Mclean; *The Guardian*, 22/08/03, feature: Lauren Zoric; *The Observer*, 01/10/00, feature; *The Wire*, 07/01, feature; *Wall Street Journal*, 18/09/00, news feature: Charles Goldsmith; *Alternative Rock Monthly* – Kim Carter; *Chicago Tribune* – Greg Kot; *USA Today* – Edna Gundersen; *MTV* – Sandy Masuo; *MTV Vibes*; *Music Central* – Tom Moon; *Wall Of Sound* – Joseph Patel; *Mr Showbiz People* – Amy Linden; *Addicted To Noise* – Laura Lee & Clare Kleinedler; *Canoe Jam Music* – John Sakamoto; *Calgary Sun* – Dave Veitch; *Toronto Sun* – Jane Stevenson, Kieran Grant, Jamie Kastner; *Ottowa Sun* – Paul Cantin; *Select*; *Vox*; Interview on *Dutch TV* at The Pink Pop Festival; *Circus* – Adrian Gregory Glover; *Mademoiselle* – Caren Myers, Kim Hughes; *The Washington Post* – Mark Jenkins; *TV2*, Chris Dusauchoit; *The Daily Egyptian*, Neil Strauss; *Entertainment Weekly*, *Promo Magazine*; *Los Angeles Times* – Robert Hilburne, Sara Scribner, C W Smets, Nisid Hajari; *Addicted To Noise* – Clare Kleinedler, Tim Gaskill, James Hunter;

JAM!; *Showbiz* – Denise Sheppard; *London Free Press* – Ian Gillespie; *The Detroit News* – Kevin Ransom, Richard Baimbridge; *Masquerade*; *Details*; *Time Out*; *Hot Press Alternative Press*, Nancy Price; *The New Music Report* – Megan Frampton; *The Rough Guide To Rock*: Ben Harrison, Michael Barclay, Fiona Coll, Saul Cozens, Leo Finlay, Scott Warnden, Julia Gordon, Lisa Robinson, Albert Clapps, Jan Sprengers. Also thanks to the following radio stations, who conducted interviews with Radiohead which have been reproduced in part in this book: BBC Radio 1, Studio Brussells Radio, KROQ and WXRK.

Particular thanks are due to the following websites: www.radiohead.com, www.climbingupthewalls.com.

All catalogue numbers are Parlophone unless stated otherwise

ON A FRIDAY TAPES

Demo Tape One [4/91]
What is it That You Say/Stop Whispering/Give It Up
No cat. number

Demo Tape Two [10/91]
I Can't/Nothing Touches Me/Thinking About You (EP version)/Phillipa Chicken/You (EP version)
No cat. number
Known as the:
'Manic Hedgehog Tape'

UK SINGLES

Drill EP [5/92]
Prove Yourself (EP version)/Stupid Car/You (EP version)/Thinking About You (EP version)
CD [CDR6312], MC [TCR6312], 12" [12R6312]
Limited edition of 3000 for each format

Creep (First Release) [9/92]
Creep/Lurgee/Inside My Head/Million $ Question
CD [CDR6078], MC [TCR6078], 12" [12R6078]
Limited edition of 6000 for each format

Anyone Can Play Guitar [2/93]
Anyone Can Play Guitar/Faithless, the Wonder Boy/Coke Babies
CD [CDR6333], MC in card case [TCR6333], 12" [12R6333]

Pop Is Dead [5/93]
Pop Is Dead/Banana Co. (acoustic)/Creep (live)/Ripcord (live)
CD [CDR6345], MC [TCR6345], 12" [12R6345]
'Banana Co.' recorded for Signal Radio, Cheshire. Live tracks from the Town and Country Club, London (14/03/93)

Creep (second release) [9/93]
Creep/Yes I Am/Blow Out (remix)/Inside My Head (live)
CD [CDR6359], MC [TCR6359], 7" clear vinyl [12R6359]
'Inside My Head' live from the Metro, Chicago (30/06/93)

Creep (US Live EP) [9/93]
Creep (acoustic)/You (live)/Vegetable (live)/Killer Cars (live)
12" numbered gatefold [12RG6359]
'Creep' recorded for KROQ radio, Los Angeles. Live tracks from the Metro, Chicago (30/06/93)

My Iron Lung CD1 [9/94]
My Iron Lung/The Trickster/Punchdrunk Lovesick Singalong/Lozenge Of Love
CD blue digipak [CDRS6394]

My Iron Lung CD2 [9/94]
My Iron Lung/Lewis (mistreated)/Permanent Daylight/You Never Wash Up After Yourself
CD red digipak [CDR6394]

My Iron Lung MC [9/94]
My Iron Lung/The Trickster/Lewis (mistreated)/Punchdrunk Lovesick Singalong
MC in card case [TCR6394]

My Iron Lung 12" [9/94]
My Iron Lung/Punchdrunk Lovesick Singalong/The Trickster/Lewis (mistreated)
12" numbered [12R6394]

High And Dry/Planet Telex CD1 [2/95]
High And Dry/Planet Telex/Maquiladora/Planet Telex (Hexidecimal mix)
CD [CDRS6405]
Hexidecimal mix by Steve Osborne for 140db

High And Dry/Planet Telex CD2 [2/95]
Planet Telex/High And Dry/Killer Cars/Planet Telex (l.f.o. jd mix)
CD [CDR6405]
l.f.o. jd mix by l.f.o., appearing courtesy of Warp Records

High And Dry/Planet Telex 12" [2/95]
Planet Telex (Hexidecimal mix)/Planet Telex (l.f.o. jd mix)/Planet Telex (Hexidecimal dub)/High And Dry
12" numbered [12R6405]
Hexidecimal Mix and Dub by Steve Osborne. l.f.o. jd Mix by l.f.o.

Fake Plastic Trees CD1, MC [5/95]
Fake Plastic Trees/India Rubber/How Can You Be Sure?
CD [CDRS6411], MC [TCRS6411]

Fake Plastic Trees CD2 [5/95]
Fake Plastic Trees/Fake Plastic Trees (acoustic)/Bulletproof . . . I Wish I Was (acoustic)/Street Spirit (fade out) (acoustic)
CD [CDR6411]
Acoustic tracks recorded live at the Eve's Club, London.

Just CD1, MC [8/95]
Just/Planet Telex (Karma Sunra mix)/Killer Cars (mogadon version)
CD [CDRS6415]
Karma Sunra mix by U.N.K.L.E.

Just CD2 [8/95]
Just/Bones (live)/Anyone Can Play Guitar (live)
CD card case plus two postcards [CDR6415]
Live tracks from the Forum, London (24/03/95)

Street Spirit CD1 [1/96]
Street Spirit (fade out)/Bishop's Robes/Talk Show Host
CD plus poster [CDRS6419]

Street Spirit CD2 [1/96]
Street Spirit (fade out)/Banana Co./Molasses
CD [CDR6419]

Street Spirit 7" [1/96]
Street Spirit (fade out)/Bishop's Robes
7" limited white vinyl [R6419]

Paranoid Android CD1 [5/97]
Paranoid Android/Polyethylene (Parts 1 & 2)/Pearly*
CD white card sleeve [CDODATAS 01]

Paranoid Android CD2 [5/97]
Paranoid Android/A Reminder/Melatonin
CD mauve card sleeve [CDNODATA 01]

Paranoid Android 7" [5/97]
Paranoid Android/Polyethylene (Parts 1 & 2)
7" clear blue vinyl with white die cut sleeve [NODATA 01]

Karma Police CD1 [8/97]
Karma Police/Meeting In The Aisle/Lull
CD white card sleeve [CDODATAS 03]
Programming for 'Meeting In The Aisle' by Henry Binns and Sam Hardaker

Karma Police CD2 [8/97]
Karma Police/Climbing Up the Walls (Zero 7 mix)/Climbing Up The Walls (Fila Brazillia Mix)
CD white card sleeve [CDNODATA 03]
Zero 7 mix by Henry Binns and Sam Hardaker at Shebang Studios. Fila Brazillia Mix by Fila Brazillia

Karma Police 12" [8/97]
Karma Police/Meeting In The Aisle/Climbing up the Walls (Zero 7 mix)
12" heavy weight vinyl [12NODATA 03]

No Surprises CD1, MC [1/98]
No Surprises/Palo Alto/How I Made My Millions
CD white card sleeve [CDODATAS 04], MC plastic case [TCNODATA 04]

No Surprises CD2 [1/98]
No Surprises/Airbag (live)/Lucky (live)
CD yellow card sleeve
[CDNODATA 04]
'Airbag' live from Berlin (3/11/97).
'Lucky' live from Florence.

No Surprises 12" [1/98]
No Surprises/Palo Alto
12" [12NODATA 04]

Pyramid Song CD1 [05/01]
Pyramid Song/The Amazing Sounds of
Orgy/Trans-Atlantic Drawl
CD [CDSFHEIT45102]

Pyramid Song CD2 [05/01]
Pyramid Song/Fast Track/Kinetic
CD [CDFFHEIT45102]

Knives Out CD1 [08/01]
Knives Out/Cuttooth/Life In A
Glasshouse (Full Length Version)/Knives
Out (Video)
CD [CDFHEIS45103]

Knives Out CD2 [08/01]
Knives Out/Worrywort/Fog/Life In A
Glasshouse (Full Length Version)
CD [CDNODATA]

Knives Out 12" [08/01]
Knives Out/Cuttooth/Life In A
Glasshouse (Full Length Version)
12" [12FHEIT45103]

There There [05/03]
There There/Paperbag Writer/Where
Bluebirds Fly
CD [CDR6608]

There There [05/03]
There There/Paperbag Writer/Where
Bluebirds Fly
12" [12R6608]

Go To Sleep CD1 [08/03]
Go To Sleep/I Am Citizen Insane/Fog
(live)
CD [CDRS6613]
'Fog' live from Paris (3/7/03).

Go To Sleep CD2 [08/03]
Go To Sleep/Gagging Order/I Am A
Wicked Child
CD [CDR6613]

Go To Sleep 12" [08/03]
Go To Sleep/I Am Citizen Insane/I Am A
Wicked Child
12" [12R6613]

2+2=5 CD1 [10/03]
2+2=5/Remyxamatosis (Christian Vogel
remix)/There There (demo)
CD [CDR6623]

2+2=5 CD2 [11/03]
2+2=5/Scatterbrain (Four Tet remix)/I
Will (1st Mix)
CD [CDRS6623]

UK ALBUMS

Pablo Honey [2/93]
You/Creep/How Do You?/Stop
Whispering/Thinking About You/
Anyone Can Play Guitar/Ripcord/
Vegetable/Prove Yourself/I Can't/
Lurgee/Blow Out
CD, LP, MC [7360]

The Bends [03/13/95]
Planet Telex/The Bends/High And Dry/
Fake Plastic Trees/Bones/nice dream/
Just/My Iron Lung/Bulletproof . . .
I Wish I Was/Black Star/Sulk/
Street Spirit (fade out)
CD, LP, MC [7372]

OK Computer [06/16/97]
Airbag/Paranoid Android/Subterranean
Homesick Alien/Exit Music (for a film)/
Let Down/Karma Police/Fitter Happier/
Electioneering/Climbing Up The Walls/
No Surprises/Lucky/The Tourist
CD, 2LP, MC [NODATA02]

Kid A [02/10/00]
Everything In Its Right Place/Kid A/The
National Anthem/How To Disappear
Completely/Treefingers/Optimistic/In
Limbo/Idioteque/Morning Bell/Motion
Picture Soundtrack
CD, 2LP, MC, [CDKIDA1]

Amnesiac [04/06/01]
Packt Like Sardines In A Crushd Tin
Box/Pyramid Song/Pulk/Pull Revolving
Doors/You And Whose Army?/I Might Be
Wrong/Knives Out/Morning
Bell/Amnesiac/Dollars And
Cents/Hunting Bears/Like Spinning
Plates/Life In A Glasshouse
CD, 2LP, MC, [CDFHEIT45101]

Hail To The Thief [09/06/03]
2+2=5/Sit Down. Stand Up/Sail To The
Moon/Backdrifts/Go To Sleep/Where I
End And You Begin/We Suck Young
Blood/The Gloaming/There There/I
Will/Punch-Up at a Wedding/
Myxamatosis/Scatterbrain/A Wolf at the
Door
CD, 2LP, MC, [5845432]
CD Limited Edition Special Packaging
[5848052]

UK PROMOS

Drill EP [5/92]
Prove Yourself (EP version)/Stupid Car/
You (EP version)/Thinking About You
(EP version)
12" white label stamped "Radiohead
12RDJ6312" [12RDJ6312]

Creep [9/92]
Creep (DJ edit)/Lurgee/
Inside My Head/Million $ Question
CD jewel case, no inlay with "special
DJ Edit sticker" [CDRDJ6078],
12" [12RDJ6078]

Pop Is Dead [5/93]
Pop Is Dead/Banana Co. (acoustic)/
Creep (live)/Ripcord (live)
CD [CDRDJ6345]

Creep [9/93]
Creep (Radio edit)
CD jewel case with no inlay
[CDRDJ6359]

Pablo Honey CD Promo [2/93]
Stop Whispering (US version)/
Prove Yourself/Lurgee
CD card sleeve with inner sleeve
[CDRDJ6369]

Pablo Honey 12" Promo [2/93]
Ripcord/Prove Yourself/Faithless, the
Wonder Boy/Stop Whispering
12" with same design as the
CD promo [12RDJ6369]

My Iron Lung [9/94]
My Iron Lung/The Trickster/
Punchdrunk Lovesick Singalong/
Lozenge of Love
12" blue sleeve with white on
black "r" globe logo [12RSDJ6394]

My Iron Lung [9/94]
My Iron Lung/Lewis (mistreated)/
Permanent Daylight/You Never
Wash Up After Yourself
12" red sleeve with white on
black "r" globe logo [12RDJ6394]

The Bends [12/94]
The Bends album
Review cassette and press
pack available for the album
from Parlophone.

High And Dry [2/95]
High And Dry
CD [HIGH1]
One-track export promo

Club Mix DJ: **Planet Telex** [2/95]
Planet Telex/Planet Telex (Hexidecimal
mix)/ Planet Telex (l.f.o. jd mix)/
Planet Telex (Trashed mix)
12" [12RDJ6405]
Hexidecimal mix by Steve Osborne.
l.f.o. jd Mix by l.f.o. Trashed mix
by Alien Beatfreak

Fake Plastic Trees [5/95]
Fake Plastic Trees (edit)/
Fake Plastic Trees
CD [CDRDJ6411]

Fake Plastic Trees [5/95]
Fake Plastic Trees/India Rubber/
How Can You Be Sure?
12" [12RDJ6411]

Just [8/95]
Just (edit)/Just
CD [CDRDJ6415]

Just [8/95]
Just/Planet Telex (Karma Sunra mix)/
Killer Cars (Mogadon version)
12" unreleased [12RDJ6415]

Street Spirit (fade out) [1/96]
Street Spirit (fade out)
CD [CDRDJ6419]

Street Spirit (fade out) [1/96]
Street Spirit (fade out)/
Bishop's Robes/ Talk Show Host
12" [12RDJ6419]

Street Spirit (fade out) [1/96]
Street Spirit (fade out)/Bishop's Robes
7" black vinyl [R6419LH]
For jukeboxes only

Paranoid Android [5/97]
Paranoid Android
*CD black and silver digipak
[CDNODATADJ 01]*

OK Computer [6/97]
OK Computer album
An Abbey Road 'studio tape'
exists as well as a press pack with CD +
video in polystyrene casing enclosed in a
'Fitter Happier' design jiffy bag.

Karma Police [8/97]
Karma Police
CD gold digipak [CDNODATADJ 03]

Karma Police [8/97]
Karma Police/Lull
7" black vinyl [NODATALH 03]
For jukeboxes only

Climbing Up The Walls
remixes [8/97]

Climbing Up The Walls (Zero 7 Mix)/
Climbing Up The Walls
(Fila Brazillia Remix)
12" [12NODATADJ 03]

Come Again Sampler 2 [8/97]
including 'Wish You Were Here' by
Sparklehorse featuring Thom Yorke on
vocals
CD [EMIDJCOM02]
6-track promo for the EMI
album *Come Again*

No Surprises [12/97]
No Surprises
CD green digipak [CDNODATADJ 04]

Optimistic [09/00]
Optimistic
CD [CDKIDA2]

Idioteque [11/00]
Idioteque
CD [CDKIDA6]

Idioteque [11/00]
Idioteque
12" [12KIDA6]

I Might Be Wrong EP [11/01]
The National Anthem/I Might Be
Wrong/Morning Bell/Like Spinning
Plates/Idioteque/Everthing In Its Right
Place/Dollars and Cents/True Love Waits
CD [CDFHEIT45104]

IMPORTANT UK
COMPILATIONS

Volume 7 [7/93]
including Stupid Car (Tinnitus Mix)
CD with book [RTM/Pinnacle 7VCD7]

Five Alive Take 3 [10/93]
including Vegetable (live)
*MC from Melody Maker (9/10/93) in card
case [Melody Maker MMMC THREE]*
'Vegetable' live from the Metro, Chicago
(30/06/93)

Brat Pack '94 [1/94]
including Banana Co. (live)
*MC from NME (29/1/94) in
card case [NME BRAT94]*
Banana Co. live from The Metro,
Chicago (30/06/93)

The Radio 1 FM Sessions [10/94]
including Just (live)
*MC from Vox (11/94) in
plastic case [VOX GIVIT8]*
'Just' live from Glastonbury
Festival '94 (6/94)

Criminal Justice! Axe the Act [8/94]
including Banana Co.
CD [Ultimate CDCRIM1]

Volume 13 [2/95]
including Nice Dream (demo)
CD with book [RTM/Pinnacle 13VCD13]

Sharks Patrol These Waters (best of
'Volume' collection) [6/95] including
Stupid Car (Tinnitus Mix)
2CD with book [RTM/Pinnacle BOVCD2]

**. . . Hold On – BBC Radio 1 FM
Sessions** [2/95]
including Street Spirit (session)
CD [MM/BBC CD 97-99]
'Street Spirit' from *Evening Session*
(14/9/94)

Clueless Soundtrack [7/95]
including Fake Plastic Trees (acoustic)
CD [Capitol CDEST 2267]
'Fake Plastic Trees' recorded live
at the Eve's Club, London.

Help EP [9/95]
Lucky/PJ Harvey – 50ft Queenie
(live)/Guru – Momentum/
Portishead – untitled
*CD in brown card sleeve
[Go! Discs HELPCD1]*

Five Alive Take 3 [3/96]
including Talk Show Host
*MC from Melody Maker (16/3/96) in card
case [Melody Maker MMMC 707]*
Studio version of 'Talk Show Host'
despite the tape being session tracks

MMMmm . . . [6/96]
including Bishop's Robes
CD from Q (7/96) [Q CDJULY 1996]

**Later Volume One :
Brit Beat** [9/96]
including The Bends (live)
CD [Island CID 8053]
Recorded for *Later, with Jools Holland* on
BBC2

**Evening Session Priority
Tunes** [12/96]
including Just (session)/Street Spirit
2CD and 2MC [Virgin VTD 88]
Recorded for BBC Radio 1 FM at Maida
Vale, Studio 4, 14/9/94

Rock The Vote [12/96]
including Planet Telex
(Hexidecimal mix)
CD [Laughing Stock LAFFCD 61 X]

Altered States [12/96]
including Planet Telex

Depthcharge Mix)
CD [Solid State SOLIDCD 4]

**Foundations: Coming Up
Off The Streets** [1/97]
including Talk Show Host
(Black Dog + Webby Mix)
CD [Feedback Communications Ltd.
FCL002CD]

**William Shakespeare's Romeo And
Juliet Soundtrack** [3/97]
including Talk Show Host
(Nellee Hooper mix)
CD [EMI 8556430]

Haute Couture [5/97]
including Banana Co.
CD from Vox (6/97) [VOX HC CD97]
incorrectly listed as 'Banana Co. (live)' on
the CD' case – it is actually the studio
version

Long Live Tibet [7/97]
including The Bends
(original 4-track demo)
CD and MC [EMI CDEMC 3768]

Round As A Pound [8/97]
including A Reminder
CD and 2000 limited 12"
[Parlophone PARLO CD 10]

**Glastonbury 97:
Mud For It** [8/97]
including Paranoid Android (live)
CD [BBC/Virgin VTCD 153]
'Paranoid Android' live from
Glastonbury Festival '97 (6/97)

Come Again [9/97]
including Wish You Were
Here by Sparklehorse featuring
Thom Yorke on vocals
2CD and 2MC [EMI COMAG001]

**hEMIstry:
A Hundred Years Of EMI** [11/97]
including Wish You Were
Here by Sparklehorse featuring
Thom Yorke on vocals
CD from Vox (11/97) [VOX EMI 100]

Tibetan Freedom Concert [11/97]
including Fake Plastic Trees (live)
2CD [EMI 7243 8 59110 2 6]
'Fake Plastic Trees' live from Tibetan
Freedom Concert, New York (7/6/97)

Brat Pack '98 [1/98]
including Meeting in the Aisle
MC in plastic case from NME
31/1/98] [NME BRAT 98]

USA SINGLES

Creep [8/93]
Creep/Faithless, The Wonder Boy
MC [Capitol]

Stop Whispering [9/93]
Stop Whispering (US Version)/
Creep (acoustic)/Pop is Dead/
Inside My Head (live)
CD (Capitol C2 7243 8 58019 2 1)
US Version remixed by
Chris Sheldon. Inside My Head
live from The Metro, Chicago
(30/06/93). Creep recorded for KROQ
radio, Los Angeles.

Stop Whispering reissue [11/93]
Stop Whispering/
Prove Yourself/Lurgee
CD (Capitol)

My Iron Lung [10/94]
My Iron Lung/The Trickster/
Punchdrunk Lovesick Singalong/
Lewis (mistreated)/
Permanent Daylight/You Never Wash Up
After Yourself
CD (Capitol)

Fake Plastic Trees [3/95]
Fake Plastic Trees/Planet Telex
(Hexidecimal mix)/Killer Cars/
Fake Plastic Trees (acoustic)
CD (Capitol C2 7243 8 58424 2 9)
Hexidecimal mix by Steve Osborne. Fake
Plastic Trees recorded live
at the Eve's Club, London.

High And Dry [2/95]
High And Dry/Fake Plastic Trees
MC (Capitol 85885374)

Just (for College) EP[10/95]
India Rubber/Maquilladora/
How Can You Be Sure?/Just (live)
CD [Parlophone RHEADU.S.1]
'Just' live from the Forum, London
(24/3/95). 'Maquiladora' mis-spelt.
Import from England.

High And Dry [2/96]
High And Dry/India
Rubber/Maquilladora/
How Can You Be Sure?/Just (live)
CD (Capitol C2 7243 8 58537 2 2)
Just live from the Forum, London
(24/3/95). 'Maquiladora' mis-spelt on inlay.

USA PROMOS

Creep [8/93]
Creep (radio edit)/Creep
CD (Capitol DPRO 79684)

Creep [8/93]
Creep/Anyone Can Play Guitar
7" green vinyl (Capitol S7 1591 B)
For jukeboxes only

Stop Whispering [9/93]
Stop Whispering (US Version)/
Stop Whispering
CD unique sleeve
(Capitol DPRO 79243)
US version remixed
by Chris Sheldon

Pablo Honey [2/93]
UK Pablo Honey album (12 tracks)
MC with 'Anyone Can Play Guitar' baby
on the cover (Capitol C4 81409)

Anyone Can Play Guitar [4/94]
Anyone Can Play Guitar
CD (Capitol DPRO 79773)

Creep acoustic [6/95]
Creep (acoustic)
CD (Capitol DPRO 79257)
'Creep' recorded for KROQ radio,
Los Angeles.

Fake Plastic Trees [3/95]
Fake Plastic Trees (edit)/
Fake Plastic Trees
CD (Capital DPRO 79567)

Fake Plastic Trees [3/95]
Fake Plastic Trees/The Bends
7" (Capitol S7 18728)
For jukeboxes only

High And Dry [2/96]
High And Dry
CD (Capitol DPRO 11225)

High And Dry [2/96]
High And Dry/Black Star
7" (Capitol S7 19017)
For jukeboxes only

Paranoid Android [5/97]
Paranoid Android
CD (Capitol)

OK Computer
personal stereo [6/97]
AIWA personal stereo with 12-track
promo 'OK Computer' cassette glued
into it

OK Computer [7/97]
OK Computer album
CD white card sleeve with black tracklisting
(Capitol CDP 7243 8 55229 2 5)

Soundtrack from the film
Nowhere (3/97)
Suede – Trash/Elastica – In the City/

How Can You Be Sure?
CD (Mercury MECD 129)

Let Down (6/97)
Let Down (edit)
CD digipak with 'Capitol' sleeve (Capitol
DPRO 7087 6 12047 2 8)

Let Down (6/97)
Let Down (edit)/Karma Police
7" [Capitol 7243 8 19624 7 3]
For jukeboxes only

Karma Police (11/97)
Karma Police
CD in jewel case
[Capitol DPRO 7087 6 12804 2 5]

Tibetan Freedom Concert (10/97)
includes Fake Plastic Trees (live)
CD eleven track promo
[Capitol DPRO 7087 6 12802 2 7]

College Karma EP (1/98)
Karma Police/Polyethylene (Parts 1 &
2)/Pearly*/A Reminder/Melatonin/
Paranoid Android
CD digipak with UK
Paranoid Android single artwork [Capitol
DPRO 7087 6 12073 2 3]

AUSTRALIA SINGLES

Many of these CDs have been
re-issued, with the label side of the CD
completely black.

Creep [9/92]
Creep (radio edit)/Lurgee/
Inside My Head/Million $ Question
CD in card sleeve [7243 8 81070 2]

Stop Whispering [2/94]
Stop Whispering (US version)/
Creep (acoustic)/Pop Is Dead/
Inside My Head (live)
CD in card sleeve [8811262]
US version remixed by
Chris Sheldon. 'Inside My Head' live
from the Metro, Chicago (30/06/93).
'Creep' recorded for KROQ radio, Los
Angeles

Anyone Can Play Guitar [6/94]
Anyone Can Play Guitar/Creep/
Pop Is Dead/Thinking About You (EP
Version)/Killer Cars (live, acoustic)
CD digipak labelled 'Australian tour
souvenir' includes tour dates inside
[8812842]

My Iron Lung [9/94]
My Iron Lung/The Trickster/Lewis
(mistreated)/Punchdrunk Lovesick
Singalong/Permanent Daylight/Lozenge
of Love/You Never Wash Up After

Yourself/ Creep (acoustic)
CD blue inlay jewel case
[7 2438 31478 2 3]
'Creep' recorded for KROQ radio, Los
Angeles.

High And Dry/
Planet Telex [2/95]
High & Dry/Planet Telex/Maquiladora/
Planet Telex (Hexidecimal mix)
CD [7243 8 82031 2 8]

Fake Plastic Trees [6/95]
Fake Plastic Trees/India Rubber/
How Can You Be Sure?
CD [7243 8 82161 2 8]

Just [4/96]
Just/Bones (live)
CD with card sleeve [7243 8 8237222]
Bones live from the Forum,
London (24/03/95)

Street Spirit (fade out) [1/96]
Street Spirit (fade out)/Bishop's Robes/
Talk Show Host/Molasses
CD [7243 8 82653 2 4]

Paranoid Android [6/97]
Paranoid Android/Polyethylene
(Parts 1 & 2)/Pearly
CD black and silver digipak like the
UK promo [7243 8 84458 2 5]
Pearly* is titled Pearly

Karma Police [7/97]
Karma Police/A Reminder/ Melatonin
CD

BELGIUM SINGLES

Live EP [5/96]
Fake Plastic Trees (live)/
Blow Out (live)/Bones (live)/
You (live)/High And Dry (live)
CD white inlay with red 'r' globe logo
[7243 8 52209 2 0]
Live tracks from Rock City, Nottingham
(5/11/95)

CANADA SINGLES

My Iron Lung [9/94]
My Iron Lung/The Trickster/
Lewis (mistreated)/Permanent Daylight/
You Never Wash Up After Yourself
CD blue digipak [EMI C2 58274]

FRANCE SINGLES

Creep [2/93]
Creep/The Benz (live)/
Prove Yourself (live)/Creep (live)
CD with 'iguana' design sleeve

[7243 8 806792 8]
Limited edition of 2000. Live tracks from
the Black Session (23/2/93). 'The Bends'
misspelt.

My Iron Lung promo [9/95]
My Iron Lung
CD card sleeve with picture [SPCD 1833]

Live A L'Astoria [9/95]
My Iron Lung (live)/
Just (live)/Maquiladora (live)
CD white inlay with blue 'r' globe symbol
[SPCD 1831]
Limited edition of 2000. Live tracks from
London's Astoria (27/5/94)

Live Au Forum [9/95]
Just (live)/Bones (live)/Planet Telex
(live)/Anyone Can Play Guitar (live)
CD white inlay with red 'r' globe
symbol [SPCD 1903]
Live tracks: Forum, London (24/3/95)

Creep promo [4/95]
Creep
CD black card sleeve with red 'r' globe
symbol [SPCD 1913]

Just promo [6/95]
Just
CD black card sleeve with gold 'r' globe
symbol [SPCD 1941]

Creep [3/96]
Creep/The Bends
CD black card sleeve with gold 'r' globe
symbol [7243 8 82633 2 0]

Karma Police [7/97]
Karma Police/Paranoid Android
CD black sleeve including French
press pack and poster [SPCD 2116]

Lucky [12/97]
Lucky/Meeting In The Aisle/
Climbing Up The Walls
(Fila Brazillia mix)
CD in card sleeve [7243 8 84980 2 9]

IRELAND SINGLES

The Bends [7/96]
The Bends/My Iron Lung (live)/
Bones (live)
CD jewel case with 'inhaler' design
cover [7243 8 83115 2 6]
Some copies play 'Planet Telex' instead of
'The Bends', and 'My Iron Lung' is
sometimes cut short. Live tracks from the
Forum,
London (24/03/95)

APAN SINGLES

Creep [1/94]
Creep / Yes I Am / Blow Out (remix) /
nside My Head (live)
CD [Toshiba-EMI TOCP 8129]
Inside My Head' live from the Metro,
Chicago (30/06/93)

Itch EP [6/94]
top Whispering (US Version) / Thinking
About You (EP Version) / Faithless, The
Wonder Boy / Banana Co. (acoustic) /
Killer Cars (live, acoustic) /
Vegetable (live) / You (live) /
Creep (acoustic)
CD including lyrics in Japanese and
English [Toshiba-EMI TOCP 8285]
Banana Co.' recorded for Signal Radio,
Cheshire. 'Creep' recorded for KROQ
adio, Los Angeles.
You' and 'Vegetable' live from
he Metro, Chicago (30/06/93)

High And Dry [4/95]
High And Dry / Planet Telex /
Maquiladora / Planet Telex
Hexidecimal Mix)
8" CD in long fold-out card sleeve
Toshiba-EMI TODP 2497]

Paranoid Android [7/97]
aranoid Android / Polyethylene (Parts 1
& 2) / Pearly* / Let Down
CD [Toshiba-EMI TOCP 40038]

**No Surprises / Running
rom Demons** EP [12/97]
No Surprises / Pearly* (remix) /
Melatonin / Meeting In The Aisle /
Bishop's Robes / A Reminder
CD in black digipak
[Toshiba-EMI TOCP 50354]
A mini-album tour souvenir
or January 1998. Pearly* remix
s very similar to original.

NETHERLANDS SINGLES

Many of these singles have been reissued

Creep [9/93]
Creep / Yes I Am / Inside My
Head (live) / Creep (acoustic)
Inside My Head' live from
the Metro, Chicago (30/06/93). 'Creep'
ecorded for KROQ radio, Los Angeles.

My Iron Lung [9/94]
My Iron Lung / The Trickster / Lewis
mistreated) / Permanent Daylight /
ou Never Wash Up After Yourself
CD blue digipak [CDRS6394]

My Iron Lung [9/94]
My Iron Lung / Permanent Daylight
CD blue card sleeve [7243 8 818032 0]

High And Dry Live
Package [2/95]
High And Dry / Creep (live) / My Iron
Lung (live) / Stop Whispering (live) /
Punchdrunk Lovesick Singalong (live)
CD white inlay with blue 'r' globe symbol
[7243 8 82094 2 7]
Live tracks from the Melkveg, Amsterdam
(2/12/94)

High And Dry [2/95]
High And Dry / Planet Telex /
Maquiladora / Killer Cars / Just
CD [7243 8 82037 2]

High And Dry [2/95]
High And Dry / Planet Telex
CD in turquoise card sleeve
[7243 8 82036 2 3]

Just [8/95]
Just / Bones (live) /
Planet Telex (Karma Sunra mix) /
Killer Cars (Mogadon Version)
CD [7243 8 82371 2 3]
Live track from the Forum, London
(24/03/95)

Street Spirit Double Pack [1/96]
contains both below CDs
CD white card box with grey 'r' globe
symbol [7243 8 82726 2 9]

Street Spirit (fade out) [1/96]
Street Spirit (fade out) / Bishop's Robes /
Talk Show Host / Molasses
CD [7243 8 82653 2 4]

2 Meter Session [1/96]
Street Spirit (fade out) /
Anyone Can Play Guitar (live) /
Bones (live) / Street Spirit (live)
CD white inlay with red 'r' globe
symbol [7243 8 82717 2 1]
Live tracks from the 2 Meter Session,
Bullit Sound Studios, 27/2/95

Street Spirit (fade out) [1/96]
Street Spirit (fade out) / Bishop's Robes
CD card sleeve [7243 8 82652 2 5]

Pinkpop Live CD [5/96]
Fake Plastic Trees (live) /
Blow Out (live) / Bones (live) /
You (live) / High & Dry (live)
CD white inlay with red 'r' globe symbol
Tracks live from Rock City, Nottingham
(05/11/95).
Note, some CDs play 'Nice Dream' (live)
instead of 'You' (live),
but are all listed as 'You' (live).

My Iron Lung [4/96]
My Iron Lung / Permanent Daylight /
Banana Co. / My Iron Lung (live)
CD [7243 8 82892 2 1]
'My Iron Lung' live from Rock City,
Nottingham (05/11/95)

Bones promo [4/96]
Bones / Black Star
CD [BONES96]

Paranoid Android [6/97]
Paranoid Android / Polyethylene
(Parts 1 & 2) / Pearly*
CD [7243 8 84123 2 2]

Karma Police promo [7/97]
Karma Police
CD [KPINT-1]

Karma Police [7/97]
Karma Police / A Reminder / Melatonin
CD digipak [7243 8 84162 2 1]

No Surprises [11/97]
No Surprises / Meeting In The Aisle / Lull
CD digipak [7243 8 84901 2 2]

NEW ZEALAND SINGLES

Itch EP [6/94]
Stop Whispering (US Version) /
Thinking About You (EP Version) /
Faithless, The Wonder Boy / Banana Co.
(acoustic) / Killer Cars (live, acoustic) /
Vegetable (live) / You (live) / Creep (acoustic)
CD with no lyrics [7243 8 55097 2 8]
'Banana Co.' recorded for Signal Radio,
Cheshire. Creep recorded
for KROQ radio, Los Angeles.
You and Vegetable live from
The Metro, Chicago (30/06/93)

OVERSEAS ALBUMS

For details on bundled EPs / singles,
see the 'Singles' section for the respective
country.

Pablo Honey USA [4/93]
plus Creep (radio edit)
CD [Capitol CDP 8140924]

Pablo Honey Canada [4/93]
plus Creep (radio edit)
CD [EMI E2 0777 7 84109 2 4]

Pablo Honey Japan [12/93]
plus Pop Is Dead / Inside My Head /
Million $ Question / Creep (live) /
Ripcord (live)
CD [Toshiba-EMI TOCP 8115]
Live tracks from the Town and Country
Club, London (14/03/93)

The Bends France [3/95]
sold with either 'Live A L'Astoria'
or 'Live Au Forum' CD
CD [8521352]

The Bends Japan [3/95]
plus How Can You Be Sure?/Killer Cars
CD [Toshiba-EMI TOCP 8489]
Early copies list 'How Can You
Be Sure?' as 'When I'm Like This'

The Bends Netherlands [5/96]
includes "Pinkpop Live CD"
CD slimline 2xCD jewel case
[7243 8 29626 2 5]

The Bends Netherlands –
Torhout Werchter Edition [5/96]
includes "Live EP"
CD slimline 2xCD jewel case
[7243 8 29626 2 5]

OK Computer Japan [5/97]
plus Polyethylene (Parts 1 & 2)/Pearly*
CD [Toshiba-EMI TOCP 50201]
Lyrics to 'Polyethylene' in booklet are
incorrect

OK Computer Germany [6/97]
includes German 'Karma Police' single
CD in box plus sticker
[7243 8 55229 2 5]
Limited edition of 10,000

IMPORTANT OVERSEAS
COMPILATIONS

Vital Brits promo [5/96]
including High And Dry/
Fake Plastic Trees/Planet Telex (live)
CD Australia
[Virgin 7243 8 14672 2 7]
Unlabelled live track from
the Forum, London (24/03/95)

2 Meter Sessies [2/96]
including My Iron Lung (live)
CD [Radio Records 481604-2]
'My Iron Lung' live from the
2 Meter Session, Bullit Sound Studios
(27/2/95)

Hot Stuff:
Live And Inedits [4/96]
including Creep (live)/
Anyone Can Play Guitar (live)
CD [EMI France SPCD 1923]
'Creep' live from London's Astoria
(27/5/94). 'Anyone Can Play Guitar' live
from the Forum, London (24/03/95)

Just Passin' Thru [5/96]
including Street Spirit (acoustic, session)
CD [HFS-99.1-96]

Recorded by WHFS-FM,
Rockville, Maryland (21/4/96)

Het Beste Uit 10 Jaar
2 Meter Sessies [1/97]
including Fake Plastic Trees (live)
CD [Radio Records]
'Fake Plastic Trees' live from the
2 Meter Session, Bullit Sound Studios
(27/2/95)

Music from the Greg Akiri movie
Nowhere [3/97]
including How Can You Be Sure?
CD [Mercury 314 534 552 2]

Tibetan Freedom Concert [11/97]
including Fake Plastic Trees (live)
3CD [Capitol]
'Fake Plastic Trees' live from
Tibetan Freedom Concert,
New York (7/6/97)

VIDEO

Rock Video Monthly: Alternative
Releases [1/94]
includes Stop Whispering
VIDEO USA [Warners 0194A]

Oxford Secret Gig 1994 [10/94]
Unknown
VIDEO UK limited to a pressing
of only 30

Live At The Astoria [3/95]
You/Bones/Ripcord/Black Star/Creep/
The Bends/My Iron Lung/Prove
Yourself/Maquiladora/Vegetable/
Fake Plastic Trees/Just/Stop Whispering/
Anyone Can Play Guitar/Street Spirit
(fade out)/Pop Is Dead/Blow Out
VIDEO UK [Pmi MVP 4914183]
Live tracks recorded at London's Astoria
(27/5/94)

Just US Promo [10/95]
Just (original version)/
Just (performance version)/
Just (narrative version)
VIDEO USA in white card slipcase
[Capitol 38249 D8922]

Rock Video Monthly: Alternative
Releases [11/95]
includes Just (original version)
VIDEO USA [Warners 1195A]

High And Dry
(US promo version) [1/96]
High and Dry (US version)
VIDEO USA in white card slipcase
[Capitol 38472 D4572]

Radiohead
In-Store Compilation [5/96]
Street Spirit (fade out)/
High And Dry (live)/The Bends (live)/
Just (performance version)/
Fake Plastic Trees/
(all tracks onwards live)
My Iron Lung/Bones/Black Star/Lucky/
Street Spirit/Planet Telex/Anyone Can
Play Guitar/Bulletproof/Blow Out/
Creep/High And Dry (US version video)
Just (narrative version)
VIDEO USA promo in full colour
cardboard box [Capitol 39641 D56717]
'High And Dry' live from
The Tonight Show with Jay Leno (3/96).
'The Bends' live from MTV's 120 Minute
(3/96).
Rest of the live tracks from
JBTV the Metro, Chicago (4/96).

Top Hits UK [7/96]
Street Spirit/Just/High And Dry
VIDEO Japan
[Toshiba-EMI TOVW 3237]

Radiohead Live
From The 10 Spot [1/98]
Airbag/Karma Police/The Bends/Exit
Music (for a film)/Talk Show Host
(audio only)/Subterranean Homesick
Alien/My Iron Lung/Climbing Up
The Walls (audio only)/Lucky/
Planet Telex/Bulletproof (audio only)/
No Surprises/Bones/
Just (audio only)/Paranoid Android/
Fake Plastic Trees/Let Down/
Street Spirit/Electioneering/
Nice Dream/The Tourist
VIDEO USA [Capitol no. cat. no.]
Live from Hammerstein Ballroom, New
York, 19/12/97

The discography was compiled by Max
Kolombos (max@kolombos.demon.co.uk)
web address: www.underworld.net/radiohead
and Richard Arthur, with thanks to:
Barbara Violani, Michael Beam, Jean-
Francois Dufour, Jonathan Moore, Cathy
Fan, Paul Prentice, Scott Minty, Izumi
Nishishita, Steve Vanderwerf, Emma
Sutcliffe, Simone de N'Ley, Cindy Moore,
Tom Angel, Roy Silverstein, Tim Lau, Ph
Tinker, Leslie Nuss, Richard Foster, Trace
Bardella, James Lambert, Jason Langer,
Christine Moon, Marie-Sophie Dion,
Olivia Trzcianowski, Mark Pytlik, Leigh
Kelsey, Clive Richardson, Ross Thompson
Evan, Emmanuel Stone, Sam Willard,
Joachim Rosenquist, Maureen Walshe,
Chris Pickering, Nigel Gleeson, Tim
Cormack, Dana Masson, Jennifer
Rakowski, Catherine Andrews, Iain
Holmes, Nick Bousfield, Alex Kent, Gary
Marshall, Nick Bousfield and many other
for moral support and help.